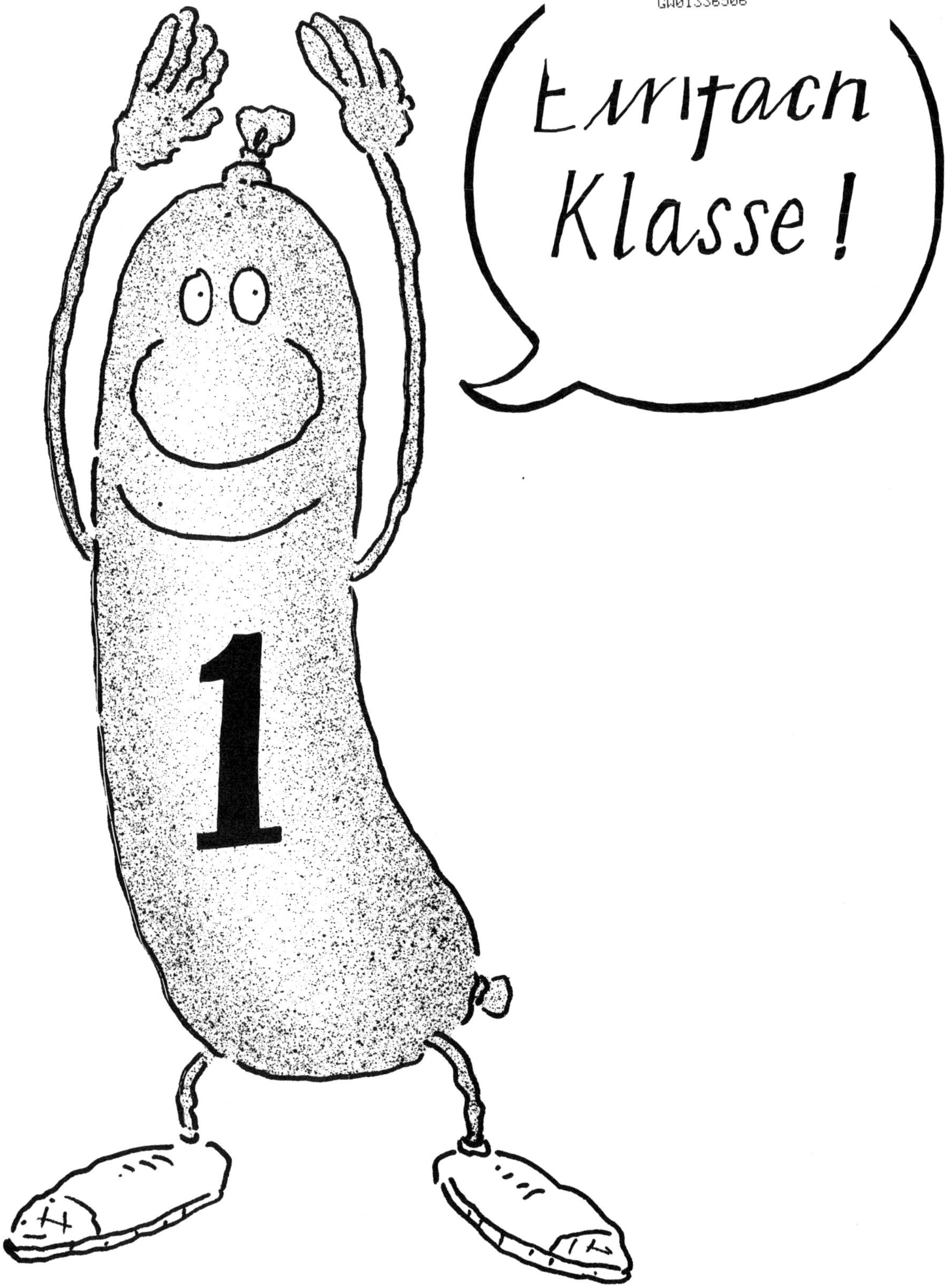
Einfach Klasse!

Inhalt

Contents

Unit			Page
1	Hallo!	Greetings	6
2	Wie heißt du?	Giving your name	8
3	Wie geht's?	Saying how you feel	9
4	Woher kommst du?	Saying where you're from	10
5	Wo ist denn das?	Explaining where you live	12
Wiederholung Eins		*Revision One*	14
6	Im Klassenzimmer	Naming things	15
7	Kleider	Saying what you're wearing	18
8	Die Farben	Describing your clothes	20
9	Jetzt gibt's Stunk!	Understanding your teacher	22
10	Hast du ...?	Asking for things	24
Wiederholung Zwei		*Revision Two*	27
11	Die Nummern	Understanding numbers	28
12	Meine Familie	Describing your family	30
13	Das Jahr in Deutschland	Understanding dates	36
14	Wie bitte?	Making yourself understood	40
Wiederholung Drei		*Revision Three*	42
15	Deutsches Geld	Using German money	43
16	In der Imbißstube	Ordering a snack	46
17	Essen in Deutschland	Food in Germany	50
18	Was ißt du gern?	Saying what you like to eat	53
19	Im Café/Restaurant	Ordering a meal	54
Wiederholung Vier		*Revision Four*	57
20	In der Stadt	Identifying places in town	58
21	Was ist denn das?	Finding your way around	62
22	Wie weit ist das?	Understanding distances	66
23	Stadtplan Cochem	Map-reading	68
24	Du, Sie und ihr	Saying 'you'	70
25	Wie komme ich am besten zu ...?	Following directions	71
Wiederholung Fünf		*Revision Five*	73
26	Wie fährt man in Deutschland?	Transport in Germany	74
27	Stadtplan Wiesbaden	Using public transport	76
28	Wohin willst du?	Saying where you're going	79
29	Ist das der Bus ...?	Getting the right bus	80
30	Wann fährt der Zug?	Asking about train times	82
31	Wie spät ist es?	Understanding times	85
32	Einmal nach Hannover, bitte	Buying tickets	88
Wiederholung Sechs		*Revision Six*	89

33	Geschäfte	Shops in Germany	90
34	Wo?	Asking where a shop is	93
35	Im Lebensmittelgeschäft	Using weights and measures	95
36	Im Kaufhaus	Buying presents	98
Wiederholung Sieben		*Revision Seven*	100
37	Schule in Deutschland	Schools in Germany	101
38	Mein Stundenplan	Explaining your timetable	105
39	Was ist dein Lieblingsfach?	Saying what subjects you like	108
40	Was ist dein Hobby?	Saying what hobbies you have	110
41	Was kannst du machen?	Saying what you can do	112
Wiederholung Acht		*Revision Eight*	114
42	Das ist mein Haus	Describing your home	115
43	Meine Tiere	Talking about pets	119
44	Wie sieht der denn aus?	Describing people	122
45	Wie man Tiere beschreibt	Describing animals	126
Wiederholung Neun		*Revision Nine*	128

Extension One	130	Extension Seven	140	Extension Thirteen	149
Extension Two	132	Extension Eight	142	Extension Fourteen	150
Extension Three	135	Extension Nine	144	Extension Fifteen	151
Extension Four	137	Extension Ten	145	Extension Sixteen	152
Extension Five	138	Extension Eleven	147		
Extension Six	139	Extension Twelve	148	German–English vocabulary	

1 ——————— Hallo! ——————— 1

Guten Tag!

Guten Morgen!

DEUTSCH — weil's einf[ach] Klasse is[t]

Tschüs!

Auf Wiedersehen!

Kapiert? (Did you catch that?)

Listen to the people on tape. They all say hello when they arrive or goodbye when they leave. Copy the grid and tick what you think each person is doing.

	Arriving	Leaving
1	✓	
2		✓
3	✓	
4	✓	
5		✓
6	✓	

Kapiert?

Now listen to these people. What time of day do you think it is in each conversation?

	Morning	Daytime	Evening
1	✓		
2	✓		
3			✓
4		✓	
5			✓
6		✓	

Und jetzt du! (Over to you!)

Greet your friend at these times:
1 2 p.m.   2 9 a.m.   3 7 p.m.   4 11 p.m.
5 11 a.m. 6 8 p.m.   7 10 a.m. 8 5 p.m.

2 Wie heißt du? 2

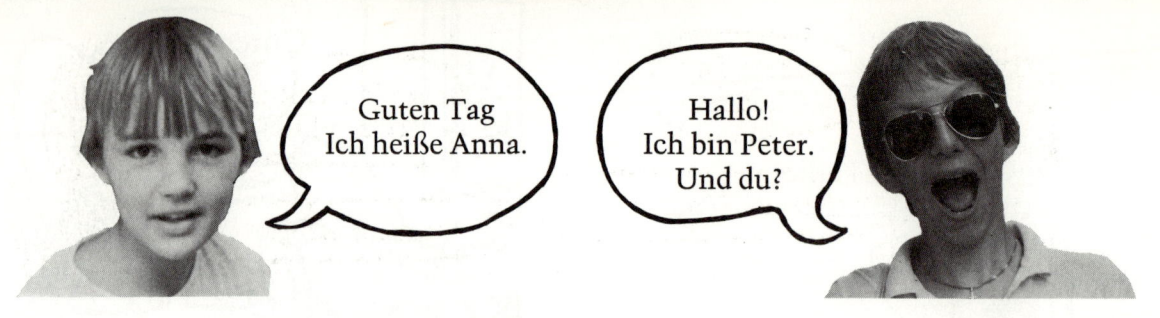

> Guten Tag
> Ich heiße Anna.

> Hallo!
> Ich bin Peter.
> Und du?

Was? (What do you want to do?)	Wie? (What do you say?)
ask someone's name	Wie heißt du?
give your name	Ich heiße Maria.
introduce a friend	Das ist Matthias.
introduce yourself	Ich bin Karl.
ask 'How about you?'	Und du?

Und jetzt du!

Greet your partner. Ask his or her name.
Give your name when asked.

Kapiert?

Und wieder du! (You again!)

In what order does Ute introduce her friends? Listen to the tape and write their names in the correct order in your book.

Can you introduce the children in all the photos on this page to your partner?

8

3 Wie geht's? 3

> Guten Tag, Thomas!

> Gut danke. Und dir?

> Hallo Markus! Wie geht's?

> Danke, auch gut.

Was?	Wie?
ask how someone is	Wie geht's?
say you're fine	Danke, gut.
ask 'And you?'	Und dir?
say you feel fantastic	Einfach Klasse!

Kapiert?

Listen to the tape and put the conversation in the right order.

Udo
1 Guten Tag, Brigitte.
2 Hallo Karin!
3 Danke, gut. Und dir?

Karin
4 Gut. Du, Udo, das ist Brigitte.
5 Hallo Udo! Wie geht's?

Now listen to the tape again and look at the photos. With your partner, try to hold the conversation you heard. It doesn't have to be exactly the same.

4　Woher kommst du?　4

Guten Tag? Wie heißt du?

Ich heiße Jörg.

Und woher kommst du?

Aus Leipzig.

i

Was?	Wie?
ask where someone comes from	Woher kommst du?
say where you come from	Ich komme aus Cardiff.
say yes	Ja.
say no	Nein.

Kapiert?

Find out:

1 the new boy's name.
2 where he is from.
3 how the girl, Uschi, feels.
4 where Uschi is from.

Listen again, and complete the sentences below using words from this box.

heiße	Neuß
Schneider	Regensburg
du	danke　Karl

Karl: Ich heiße ____ _____. Und du?
Uschi: Ich _____ Uschi. Wie geht's?
Karl: Gut, _____, und dir?
Uschi: Auch gut. Sag' mal, Karl, woher kommst du?
Karl: Ich komme aus ____. Und du?
Uschi: Na, aus Ulm, natürlich. Bist du doof?

Woher kommt der Wagen?

Can you work out where these cars come from? They are all German, and the first few letters on a German number-plate tell you what town the car is from.

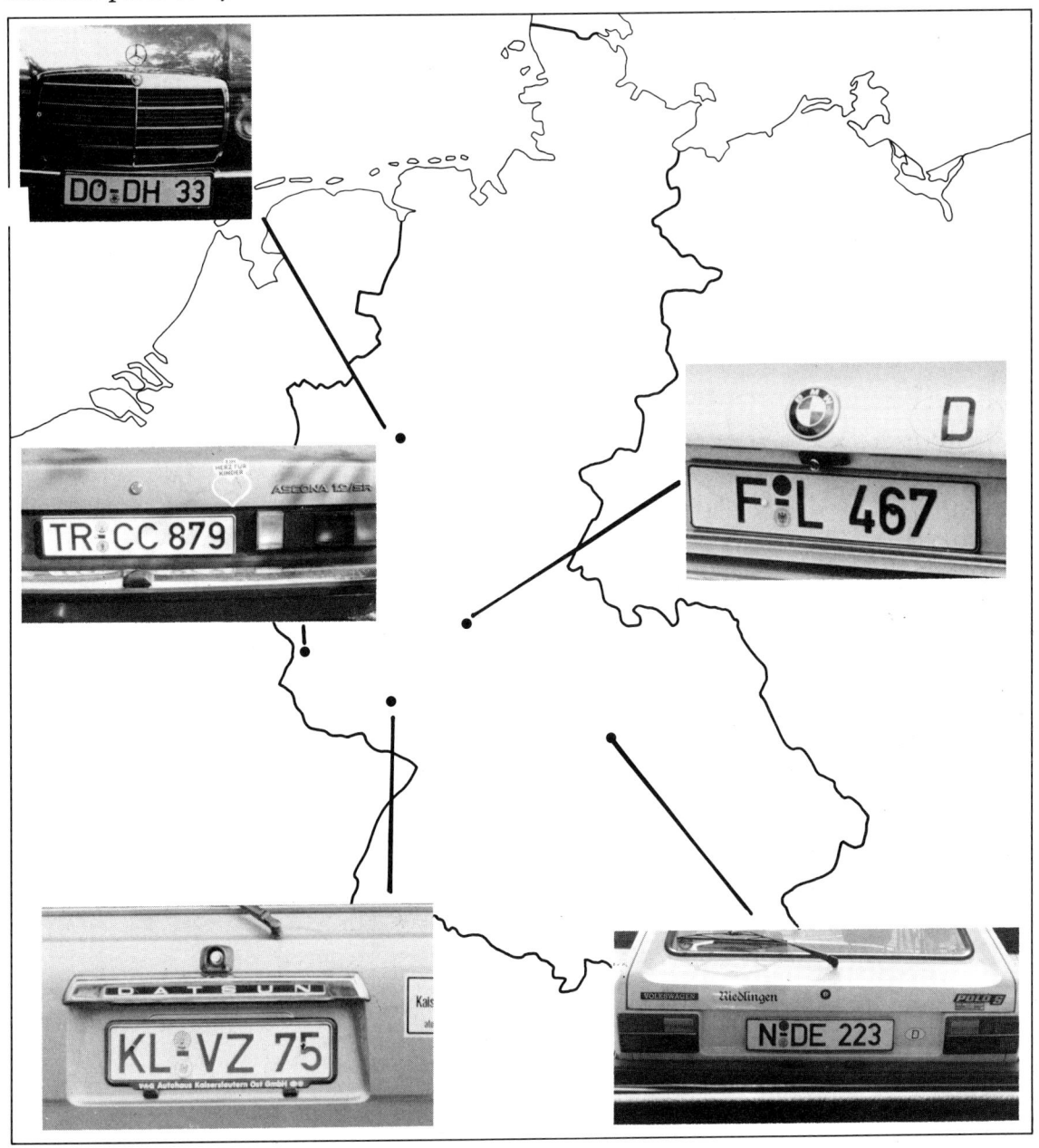

Towns	
DO	Dortmund
F	Frankfurt
KL	Kaiserslautern
N	Nürnberg
TR	Trier

1 Der Mercedes kommt aus _____.
2 Der Polo kommt aus _____.
3 Der Datsun kommt aus

_____.

4 Der Ascona kommt aus _____.
5 Der BMW kommt aus _____.

11

5 — Wo ist denn das? — 5

Was?	Wie?
ask where a place is	Wo ist (denn) das?
say what part of the country it is in	Das ist in Nordengland. Das ist in Südwales. Das ist in Ostschottland. Das ist in Westirland. Das ist in Südwestdeutschland. Das ist in Nordostösterreich.

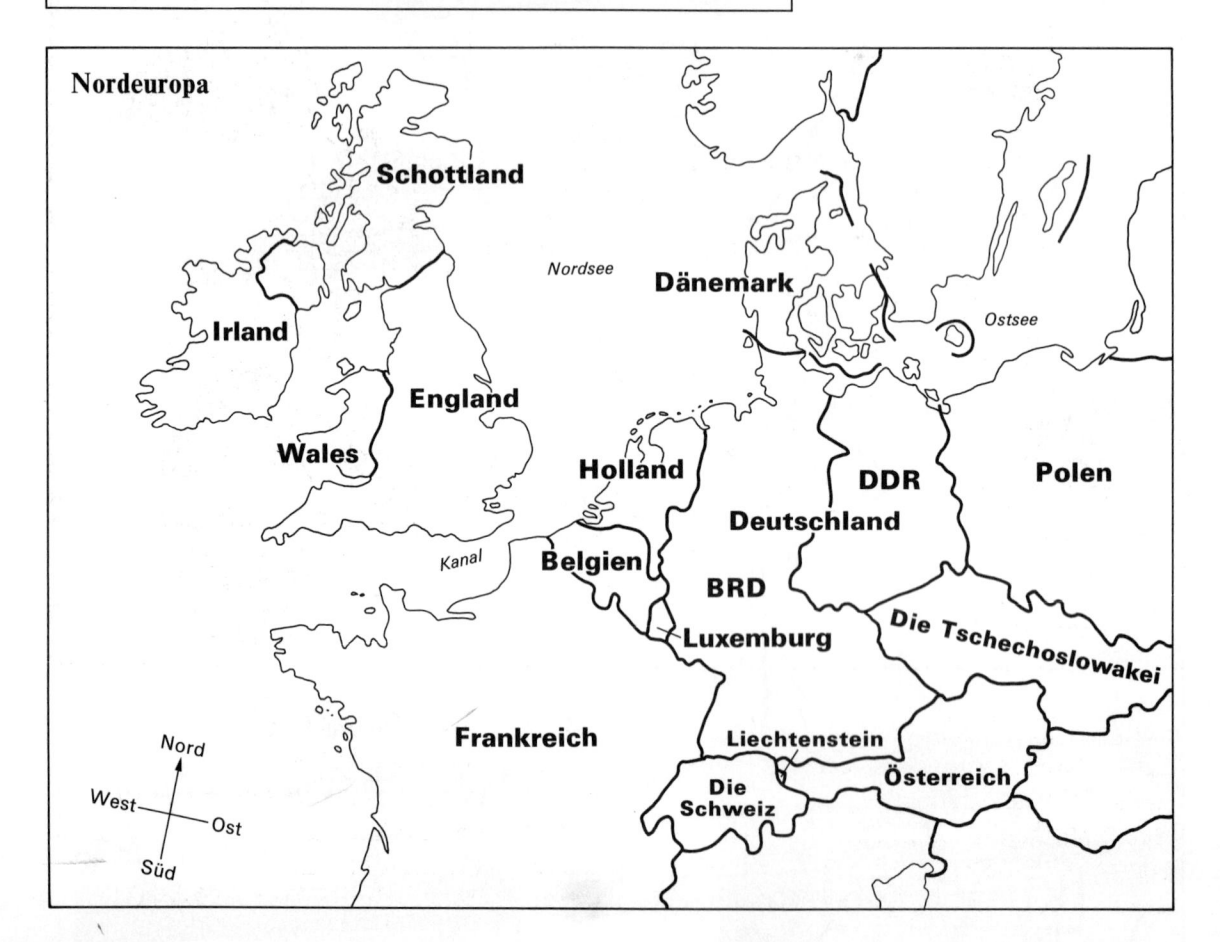

Nordeuropa

Schottland
Nordsee
Dänemark
Ostsee
Irland
England
Wales
Holland
DDR
Polen
Kanal
Belgien
Deutschland
Luxemburg
BRD
Die Tschechoslowakei
Frankreich
Liechtenstein
Die Schweiz
Österreich

Nord / West — Ost / Süd

Kapiert?

Two children are on an exchange visit to Austria. They are being interviewed by the local radio station in Linz. See if you can find out these things:

1. their names
2. where each of them comes from
3. exactly where those places are

Wo bist du?

These children in West Germany are trying to phone their friends, but they keep getting wrong numbers. Follow the lines to find out where they live, then complete the conversations as they find out who they are talking to.

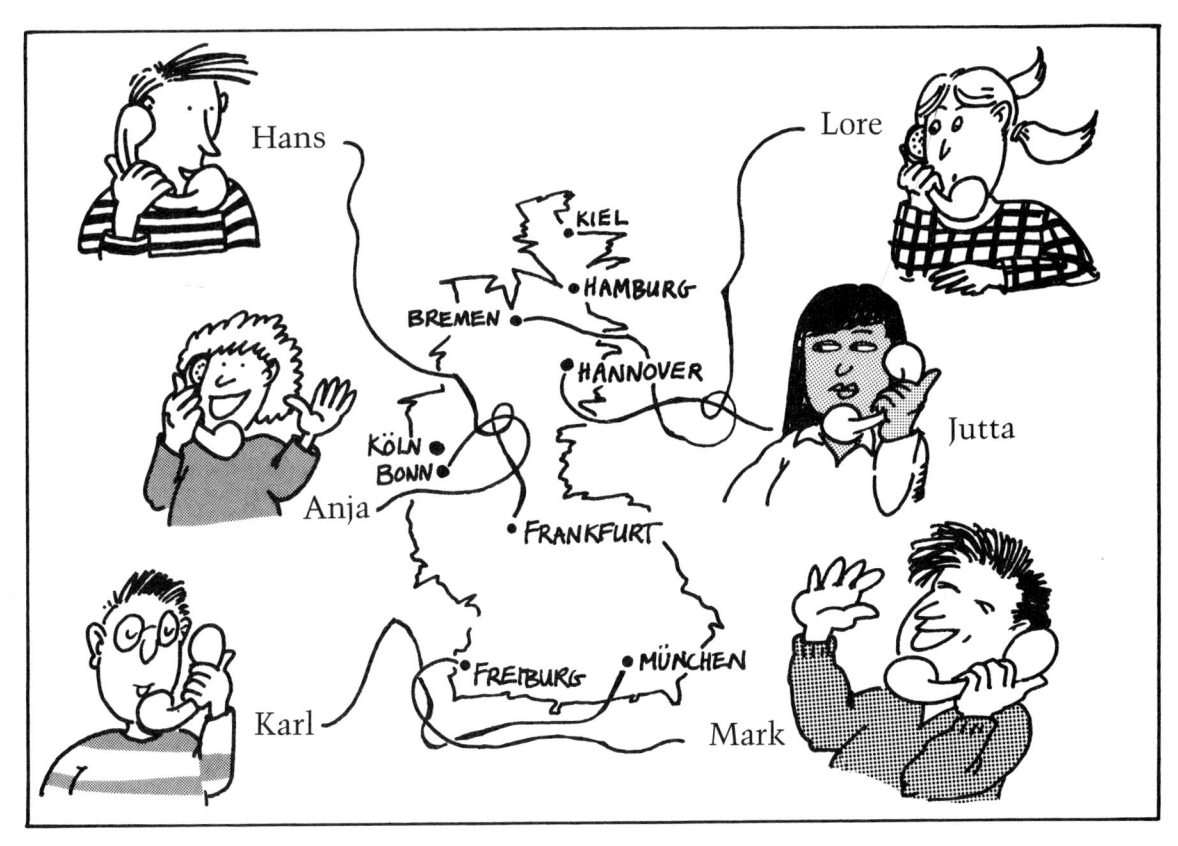

Hans: Hallo. Ist das Mark?
Lore: Nein, ich heiße Lore.
Hans: Wo bist du, Lore?
Lore: Ich bin in _____.
Hans: Wo ist denn das?
Lore: Das ist in Norddeutschland.

Karl: Hallo. Ist das Jutta?
Mark: Nein, ich heiße ____.
Karl: Wo ____ __, Mark?
Mark: Ich ___ __ ___ ___.
Karl: __ ___ denn ___?
Mark: Das ___ __ Süddeutschland.

Und jetzt du!

Partner **A** is Anja.

You want to talk to Lore, but you get the wrong number.
1 Ask if it is Lore.
3 Ask where Jutta is.
5 Ask where that is.

Partner **B** is Jutta.

Anja rings you by mistake. She really wants Lore.
2 Say you're not Lore, but Jutta.
4 Say you are in Hannover.
6 Say that's in North Germany.

Wiederholung Eins (Revision 1)

> Liebe Inge,
> Ich bin jetzt in Oberammergau. Das ist in Süddeutschland.
> Meine neue Adresse ist:
> Festspielweg 37
> 8103 OBERAMMERGAU
> Viele Grüße
> Gabi

Frl
Inge Schmidt
Karlstr. 9
6500 Mainz

Das ist neu	This is new
liebe	dear
jetzt	now
meine neue	my new
Adresse	address
viele Grüße	best wishes
Frl. (Fräulein)	Miss

Ja oder nein?

1 Inge ist in Mainz.
2 Gabi ist in Mainz.
3 Inges Adresse ist Karlstraße 37.
4 Oberammergau ist in Norddeutschland.
5 Gabis Adresse ist Festspielweg 37.

Und jetzt du!
Bild

Name	Petra	Jörg	Günther	Marika	Stefan
Wohnort	Lübeck	Leipzig	Köln	Dortmund	München
In	Norddeutschland	Ostdeutschland	Westdeutschland	Westdeutschland	Süddeutschland

Introduce each of these people to your friend. *Example:* Das ist Petra.
Sie kommt aus Lübeck.
Das ist in Norddeutschland.

Und wieder du!

Partner **A** ist Petra.   Partner **B** ist Jörg.

1 Say hello.
3 Ask his name.
5 Ask where he is from.
7 Ask where that is.

2 Say hello.
4 Give your name.
6 Say where you are from.
8 Say where that is.

Now pretend to be two other people from the chart above. **B** starts this time.

NOW YOU ARE READY FOR WAYSTAGE 1.

6 Im Klassenzimmer 6

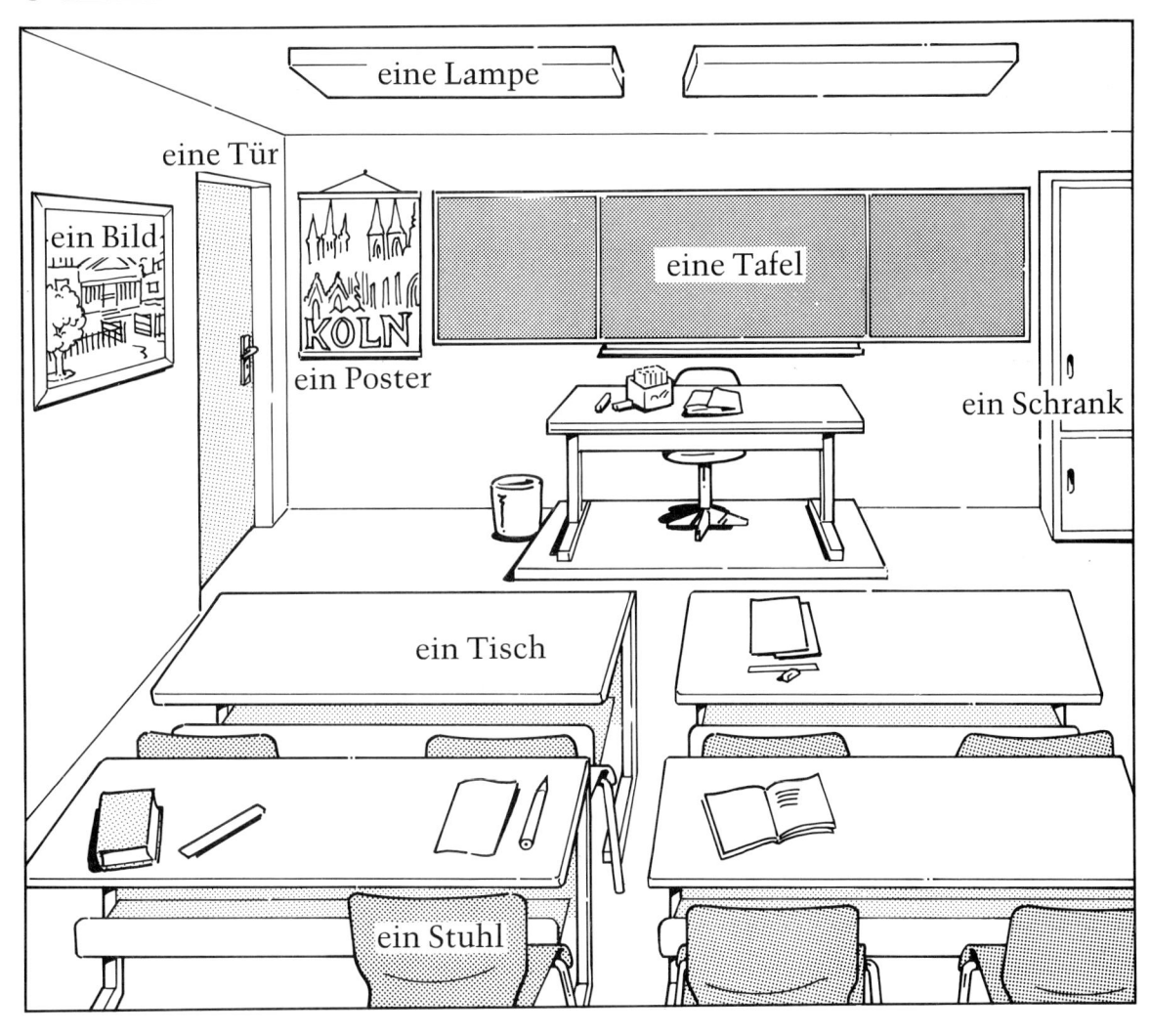

(Classroom illustration with labels:)
- eine Lampe
- eine Tür
- ein Bild
- ein Poster
- eine Tafel
- ein Schrank
- ein Tisch
- ein Stuhl

Was?	Wie?
ask what something is	Was ist das?
	Was ist denn das?
ask its German name	Wie heißt das auf deutsch?
say what it is	Das ist ein ____.
	Das ist eine ____.

Und jetzt du!

Ask your partner to name everything you point to in the classroom.

Kannst du zeichnen?

Draw your classroom and label everything you can in German.

Nein, du Idiot!

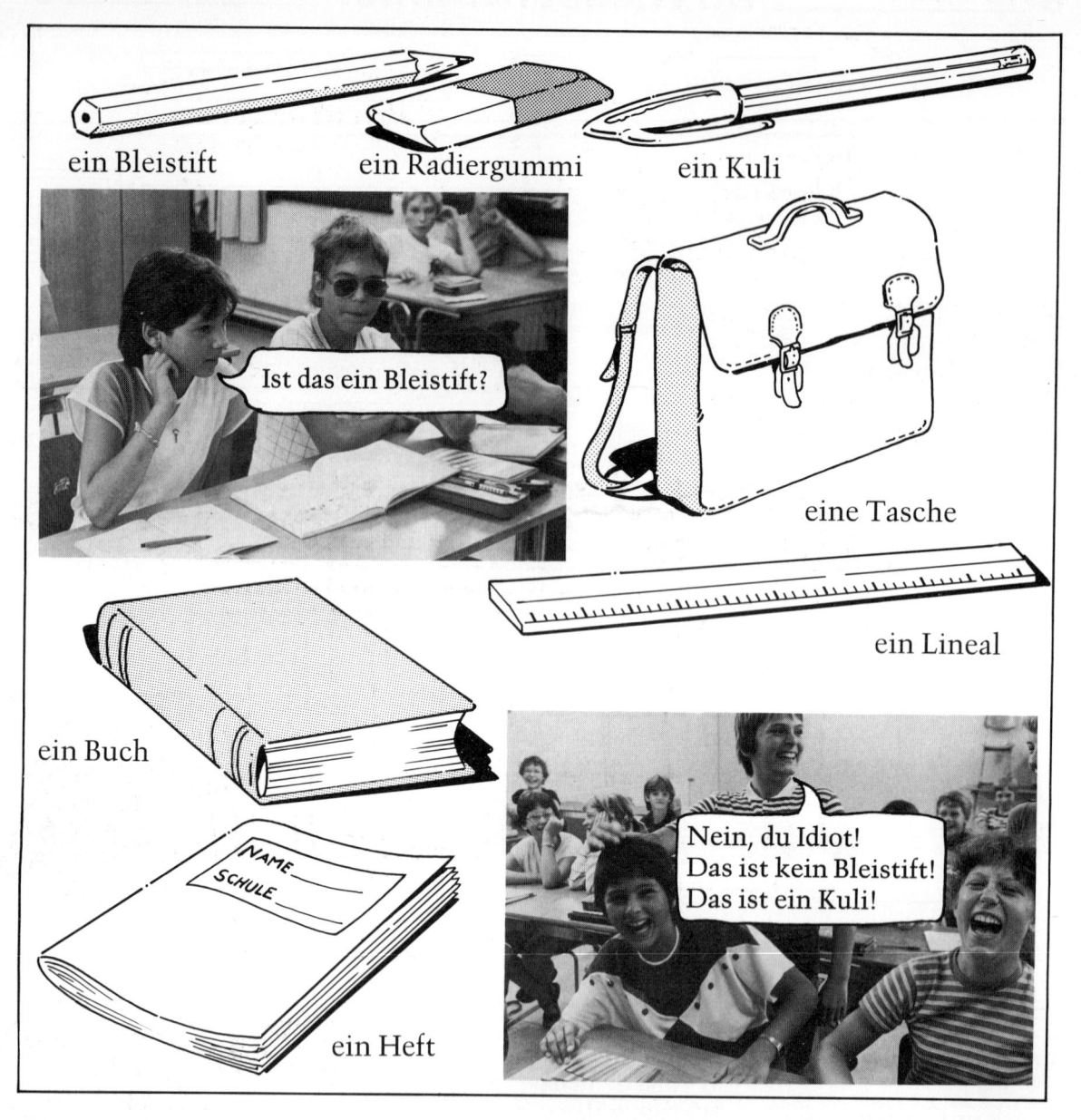

ein Bleistift

ein Radiergummi

ein Kuli

Ist das ein Bleistift?

eine Tasche

ein Lineal

ein Buch

ein Heft

Nein, du Idiot!
Das ist kein Bleistift!
Das ist ein Kuli!

Und jetzt du!

Think up silly questions in German to ask your friend. See if you can answer his or her questions.

Kannst du zeichnen?

Draw and label the contents of your school bag. Draw anything you've forgotten to bring in a different colour!

ACHTUNG!

German nouns (names of things) have gender.

Each word is masculine, (m.) – **der** words,
feminine (f.) – **die** words,
or neuter (n.) – **das** words.

To find out which is which, look in the vocabulary at the back of the book. Nouns have **der**, **die** or **das** in front of them.

Mein Tisch

Hallo! Ich heiße Gert. Und du? Ich komme aus Worms, in Deutschland.

Hier ist mein Tisch im Klassenzimmer.

Hier sind mein Kuli, mein Bleistift, mein Lineal und mein Radiergummi.

Das ist mein Deutschheft.

Das ist mein Deutschbuch.

Das ist meine Tasche.

Was?	Wie?
say 'This is my ____.'	Das ist mein ____. (m.) & (n.)
	Das ist meine ____. (f.)
ask 'Is this your ____?'	Ist das dein ____? (m.) & (n.)
	Ist das deine ____? (f.)

Das ist wohl dein Spitzer.

Und jetzt du!

Describe what is on your desk to your partner. Use **mein** and **meine**.

Und wieder du!

Ask your partner if various items belong to him or her.

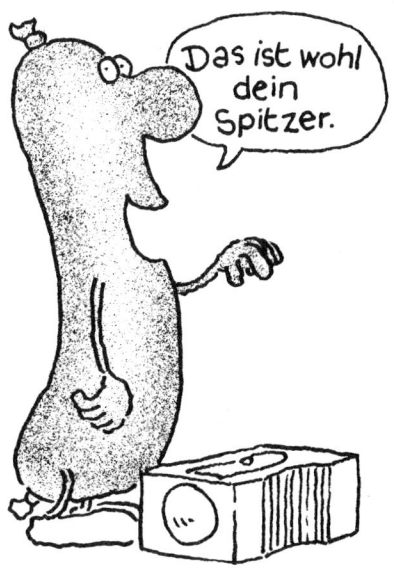

7 Kleider 7

George
- ein Pullover
- ein Rock
- ein Schottenrock
- Strümpfe
- Schuhe

Kurt
- eine Mütze
- ein Hemd
- eine Krawatte
- eine Jacke
- eine Hose
- Socken

Ergänze (Complete)

1 George hat einen P_____ an.
 (George is wearing a pullover.)
2 Kurt hat eine J____ an.
3 ____ hat einen Rock an.
4 ____ hat eine Hose an.
5 ____ hat Strümpfe an.
6 ____ hat Socken an.
7 George ___ Schuhe an.
8 Kurt ___ ein Hemd an.
9 Kurt ___ eine Mütze auf.

ACHTUNG!
Use 'hat ... an' when something is worn on the body.
Use 'hat ... auf' when something is worn on the head.

Das ist meine Freundin Wursteline. Sie hat einen Rock und einen Pullover an und eine Mütze auf.

Kannst du zeichnen?

Draw a person wearing some of these clothes.
Label the clothes.
Say what the person has on.

Martina

eine Bluse
ein Anorak
Handschuhe
Jeans
Stiefel

Sabine

eine Jacke
ein Kleid
eine Strumpfhose

Ergänze

1 Martina hat einen A_____ an.
2 Sabine hat eine J____ an.
3 Martina hat H_____ an.
4 ____ hat ein Kleid an.
5 Martina hat eine J____ an.
6 Sabine hat eine S_____ an.
7 ____ hat Stiefel an.

Kannst du zeichnen?

Draw yourself in your everyday clothes (not school clothes).

Label the clothes.

Say what you are wearing in the picture. Use **'Ich habe ____ an'**.

Und jetzt du!

Decribe one of the four people on these two pages to your partner. Your partner must close his or her book and work out who you are describing. Take turns.

8 Die Farben 8

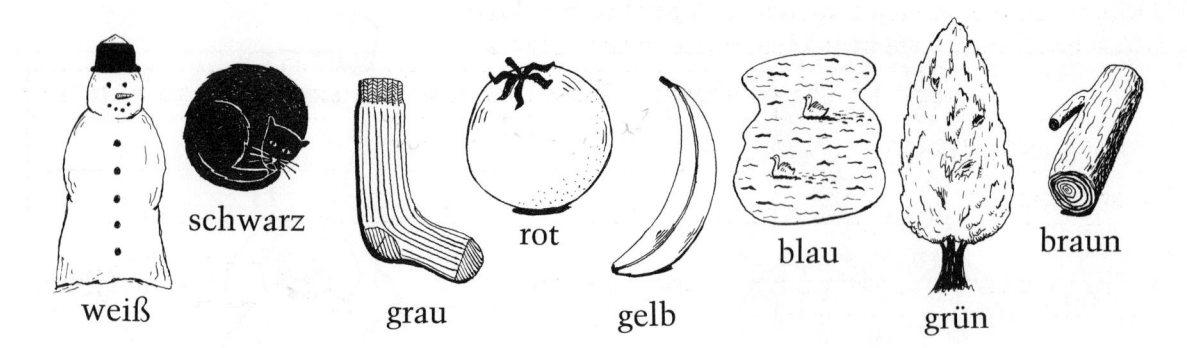

schwarz
weiß
grau
rot
gelb
blau
grün
braun

	Was?	Wie?
	say what you have on	Ich habe ein ____ an. Ich habe eine ____ an. Ich habe einen ____ an.
	say what a boy or man has on	Er hat ein ____ an. Er hat eine ____ an. Er hat einen ____ an.
	say what a girl or woman has on	Sie hat ein ____ an. Sie hat eine ____ an. Sie hat einen ____ an.

Birgits Kleider

Hallo! Ich heiße Birgit. Ich komme aus Aurich, in Norddeutschland. Und du?

Ich habe eine Mütze auf und einen Pullover, eine Hose, Socken und Schuhe an. Und du?

Mein Hut ist rot und blau.
Mein Pullover ist schwarz.
Meine Hose ist gelb.
Meine Socken sind weiß.
Meine Schuhe sind braun.
Und meine Tasche ist sehr bunt – grau, rot, orange, gelb, grün, blau und violett.
Wie sind deine Kleider?

Ist das deine Tasche?

Kapiert?

a Annemarie and Christoph are being interviewed for a programme on teenage fashions. Copy this grid. First tick what they are wearing, then write in the colours.

	Rock	Jeans	Pullover	Bluse	Krawatte	Socken	Schuhe	Mütze
Annemarie	✓ grün			weiß	schwarz	schwarz	schwarz	
Christoph		blau	rot			grau	schwarz	rot

b The interviewer is asking Annemarie questions. Answer for her.

ist – is
sind – are

1 Wie ist dein Rock? — Mein Rock ist grün.
2 Wie ist deine Bluse? — Meine Bluse ___ ___.
3 Wie ist deine Krawatte? — Meine Krawatte ___ ___.
4 Wie sind deine Socken? — Meine Socken sind ___.
5 Wie sind deine Schuhe? — Meine Schuhe ___ ___.

c How does Christoph answer?

Dein in the question becomes **mein** in the answer.
Deine in the question becomes **meine** in the answer.

1 Wie sind deine Jeans?
2 Wie ist dein Pullover?
3 Wie ist deine Mütze?
4 Wie sind deine Socken?
5 Wie sind deine Schuhe?

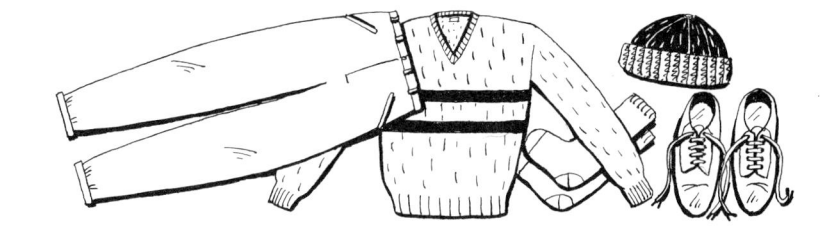

Und jetzt du!

Ask each other what colour your clothes are. Answer.

Rätsel (Puzzle)

Can you unjumble the words and find the password in the box? They are all articles of clothing.

1 UHHCS — Schuh
2 AJNSE — Jeans
3 ILKED — Kleid
4 SOEHRMUFSTP — Strumpfhose
5 OESH — Hose
6 EWAARTKT — Krawatte
7 DHEM — Hemd

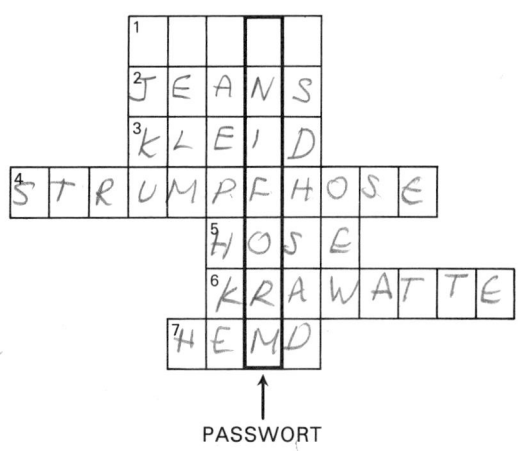

PASSWORT

21

9   Jetzt gibt's Stunk!   9

Michael is generally late for lessons and never has all his school things.

die Lehrerin

Du kommst zu spät, Michael. Wo warst du?

Bei Frau Braun.

Wo ist denn deine Krawatte?

Zu Hause.

So, und dein Kuli?

In meiner Tasche.

Gut, und dein Deutschbuch?

Ich weiß nicht.

Typisch. Und dein Heft?

Auf dem Tisch.

Und dein Lineal und dein Radiergummi sind auf dem Boden.

Oh, danke.

Information

Michael must be British. German children do not have a school uniform. Their teachers do not talk about their clothes.

Kapiert?

1. Why is Maria late?
2. Where is her jacket?
3. Where is her tie?
4. Where is her bag?
5. Where is her German book?
6. Where is her exercise book?
7. Where is her pen?
8. Where is her pencil?

Das ist neu

Du kommst zu spät.	You're late.
Wo warst du?	Where have you been?
bei Frau Braun	with Mrs Braun
zu Hause	at home
in meiner Tasche	in my bag
auf dem Tisch	on the table
auf dem Boden	on the floor
auf dem Stuhl	on the chair
Ich weiß nicht.	I don't know.

Und jetzt du!

Ask each other where your things are.
Answer truthfully.

Mach das mal!

Steh auf!   Steht auf!   Komm her!   Geh zu ...

Setz dich!   Setzt euch!   Mach die Tür auf!   Mach das Fenster zu!

Fang an!   Hör auf!   Nicht vergessen!

Lauter, bitte!    Seid leise! / Leiser, bitte! / Ruhe bitte!   Schnell!   Langsam!

Hört zu!    Schreib den Titel!   Schreib das Datum!   Dreh dich um!

Hast du...? 10

...sation

...:	Du, Joachim, hast du einen Radiergummi?
Joachim:	Nein, tut mir leid, ich habe keinen.
Felix:	Peter, hast du einen Radiergummi?
Peter:	Wie? Einen Radiergummi? Nein.
Felix:	Susi, sag' mal, hast du einen Radiergummi?
Susi:	Nein, ich habe keinen Radiergummi. Frag' mal Laura.
Felix:	Hast du einen Radiergummi, Laura?
Laura:	Ja sicher. Bitte.
Felix:	Danke schön.

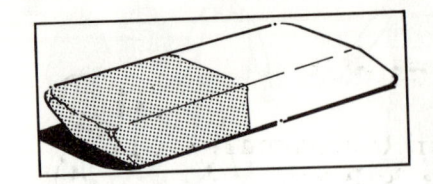

Ja oder nein?

1 Felix hat einen Radiergummi.
2 Joachim hat keinen Radiergummi.
3 Peter hat einen Radiergummi.
4 Susi hat keinen Radiergummi.
5 Laura hat einen Radiergummi.

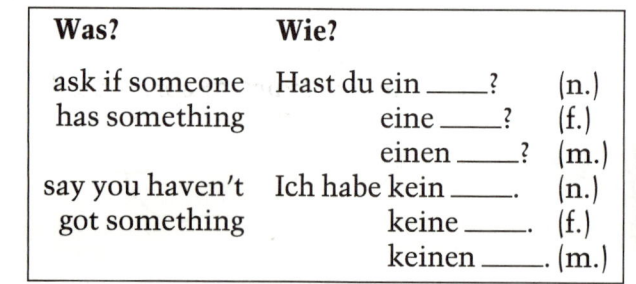

Was?	**Wie?**
ask if someone has something	Hast du ein ____? (n.) eine ____? (f.) einen ____? (m.)
say you haven't got something	Ich habe kein ____. (n.) keine ____. (f.) keinen ____. (m.)

Und was hast du heute vergessen?
(And what have you forgotten today?)

The list shows what Felix brought to school today and what he forgot. Look at the examples, then pretend to be Felix and tell your teacher what you have got.

Beispiel (Example):

die	Tasche	ja
der	Kuli	nein

Ich habe eine Tasche.
Ich habe keinen Kuli.

der	Kuli	ja
die	Tasche	ja
das	Matheheft	ja
der	Radiergummi	nein
das	Lineal	nein

das	Deutschbuch	ja
der	Bleistift	ja
die	Krawatte	nein
die	Jacke	nein
das	Sporthemd	ja

der	Pullover	ja
das	Englischheft	nein
die	Mütze	nein
der	Spitzer	ja

Und jetzt du!

Ask each other what you have brought to school today.
Be honest! Use '**Hast du _____?**'

Ist das deins?

Ist das dein Radiergummi?
– Nein, der ist Peters.

Ist das Karls Lineal?
– Nein, das ist Bodos.

Ist das mein Kuli?
– Nein, der ist Julias.

Ist das Inges Tasche?
– Nein, die ist Dieters.

Das ist nicht dein Buch, oder?
– Doch, das ist meins.

ACHTUNG!

There are three words for 'it' on this page. Can you spot them?

der for a **der** word
die for a **die** word
das for a **das** word

Doch!

Doch! means 'yes'.
Use it to mean 'Oh yes it is!'
when you are contradicting someone.

Und jetzt du!

Katrin

Kurt

Marlis

Bodo

Work in groups of three or four. Each of you must pretend to be one of the people on the left. Work out what belongs to you, then ask who owns what, and answer their questions. Katrin starts.

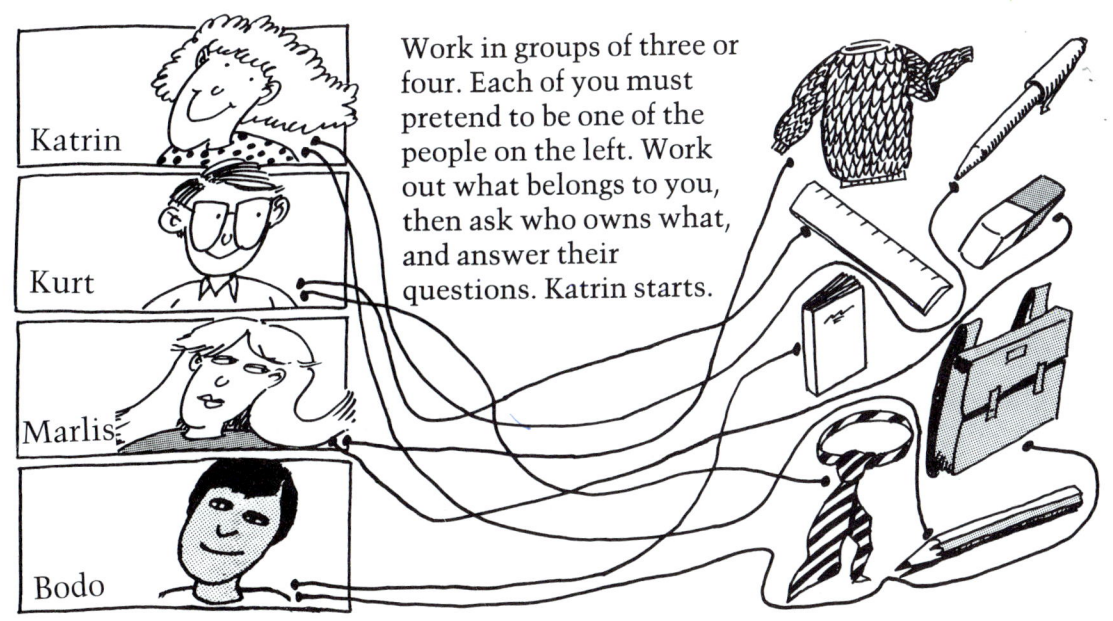

Wem gehört das?

Herr Becker: Du, Sabine, ist das dein Bleistift?
Sabine: Ja, danke.

Herr Becker: Ist das dein Radiergummi?
Sabine: Ja.
Herr Becker: Hier bitte.
Sabine: Danke.

Herr Becker: Uli, ist das dein Kuli?
Uli: Nein, der ist Karins.
Herr Becker: Ach so.

Uli: Du, ist das deins?
Karin: Ja.

Herr Becker: Sag mal, Sabine, ist das deine Tasche?
Sabine: Nein, die ist Petras.

Kapiert?

Who owns these things?

Katya?
Petra?
Joachim?

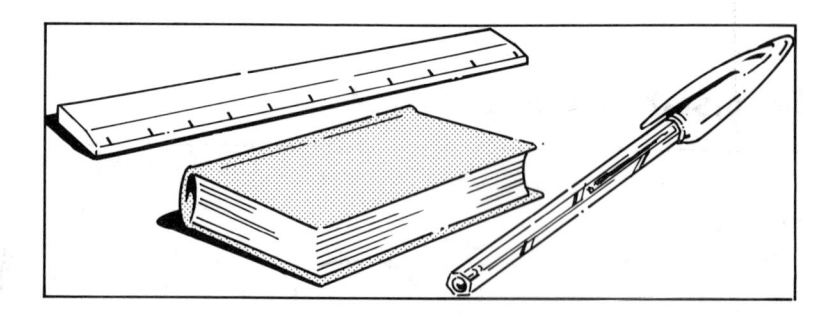

Was?	Wie?
ask who something belongs to	Wem gehört das?
say you don't know	Ich weiß nicht.
ask 'Is this yours?'	Ist das deins?
	Ist das dein _____?
	Ist das deine _____?
attract a friend's attention	Du!
	Sag mal!
hand something over	Hier bitte.
say thank you	Danke.

Und jetzt du!

Pick up different things in the classroom. Ask each other who owns them. Answer truthfully.

Wiederholung Zwei

◉ Kapiert?

Copy the grid. As you listen, tick what each pupil has left at home.

Name	Tasche (f.)	Heft (n.)	Kuli (m.)	Bleistift (m.)	Lineal (n.)	Radiergummi (m.)
Uwe						
Paul						
Lena						
Sonja						
Axel						
Monika						

Kannst du Deutsch schreiben?

Write sentences about the pupils in the grid above. Say what they have and have not got in school today.

Beispiel: Axel hat eine Tasche. Paul hat keinen Kuli.

ACHTUNG!
After '**hat**' use
ein/kein with **das** words
eine/keine with **die** words
einen/keinen with **der** words

Kannst du Deutsch lesen?

> Frankfurt, den 20.9.
>
> Lieber John,
> Hier ist mein Foto. Ich bin da im Klassenzimmer. Das ist meine Freundin Sabine. Ich habe keine Schuluniform. Im Foto habe ich ein Kleid an. Das Kleid ist gelb und schwarz. Sabine hat Jeans und ein Hemd an.
> Hast Du ein Foto von Dir in Deiner Uniform?
> Deine Paula.

Answer these questions:

1. Does Paula wear a uniform?
2. What colour is her dress?
3. What is her friend wearing?
4. What would Paula like?

🗣 Plappermaul (Chatterbox)

Make up as many conversations as you can with your partner, using this grid:

A	Ist das dein Kuli?	Sag mal! Ist das dein Heft?	Du, Hans! Ist das deine Tasche?	Marika! Ist das deine Jacke!
B	Ja, danke.	Nein, Karls.	Nein, Inges.	Oh ja.
A	Bitte.	Hier bitte.	Ach so.	Oh.

NOW YOU ARE READY FOR WAYSTAGE 2.

Die Nummern

0	null	11	elf
1	eins	12	zwölf
2	zwei	13	dreizehn
3	drei	14	vierzehn
4	vier	15	fünfzehn
5	fünf	16	sechzehn
6	sechs	17	siebzehn
7	sieben	18	achtzehn
8	acht	19	neunzehn
9	neun	20	zwanzig
10	zehn		

Lotto!

Write down any six numbers between 1 and 10. If your teacher reads out a number that you have written, cross it out. When you have crossed out all six numbers, shout '**fertig!**'. Your teacher will tell you to read back your numbers in German, to check that you are the winner.

Now try with numbers between 1 and 20.

Telefonnummern

German phone numbers can be given figure by figure, as in English, or in pairs like this: 23–45–67. Read the numbers below to your partner number by number:

a 370216   **b** 984351   **c** 628064
d 753204   **e** 654197   **f** 345982

Your teacher will read out these phone numbers in random order. Write the numbers **a–f** in the order your teacher reads the numbers.

Und jetzt du!

Dictate your phone number to a partner, who writes it down. See if he or she gets it right. (If you are not on the phone, make up a number.)

Wie alt bist du?

20 zwanzig	26 sechsundzwanzig	50 fünfzig
21 einundzwanzig	27 siebenundzwanzig	60 sechzig
22 zweiundzwanzig	28 achtundzwanzig	70 siebzig
23 dreiundzwanzig	29 neunundzwanzig	80 achtzig
24 vierundzwanzig	30 dreißig	90 neunzig
25 fünfundzwanzig	40 vierzig	100 hundert

Kapiert?

Wie alt sind die Kinder?
Hör gut zu!

Günther ist zwölf.
Heidi ist ___.
Max ist _____.
Rudi ist _____.
Und Klaus? Er ist _____.
Und Sabine? Sie ist _____.
Und Ingrid? ___ ___ ____.

Und jetzt du!

Ask your friends how old they are. Note down their answers to tell your teacher.

Wie?	Was?
ask a person's age	Wie alt bist du?
	Wie alt ist er?
	Wie alt ist sie?
answer	Ich bin 13.
	Er ist 24.
	Sie ist 7.

12 Meine Familie 12

> München, den 6.11.
>
> Lieber John,
> Hier ist ein Foto von meiner Familie. Mein Vater heißt Georg. Er ist vierzig Jahre alt. Meine Mutter heißt Verena. Sie ist einundvierzig. Mein Bruder Volker ist acht und meine Schwester Christel ist zehn. Ich bin zwölf Jahre alt. Wer ist in Deiner Familie?
> Viele Grüße
> Paul

Ergänze

1 Paul ist ___ Jahre alt.
2 Sein Bruder heißt ___.
3 Volker ist ___ Jahre alt.
4 Christel ist seine ___.
5 Sie ist ___ Jahre alt.
6 Pauls Vater heißt ___.
7 Er ist ___ Jahre alt.
8 Seine Mutter, Verena, ist ___ Jahre alt.

Das ist neu	
Lieber John	Dear John
Liebe Sue	Dear Sue
hier	here
von	of
Jahre alt	years old
wer?	who?
Viele Grüße	Best wishes
sein	his

Und jetzt du!

Draw your family and describe it to a friend in German. Better still, bring in a photo and describe it.

	Masculine	Feminine
the	der Vater	die Mutter
a	ein Vater	eine Mutter
my	mein Vater	meine Mutter
your	dein Vater	deine Mutter
his	sein Vater	seine Mutter
her	ihr Vater	ihre Mutter
no	kein Vater	keine Mutter

Do you notice anything?
What extra letter do you need before a feminine word?

What do you think will happen to these?

	der Bruder	die Schwester
the	der Bruder	die Schwester
a	? Bruder	? Schwester
my	? Bruder	? Schwester
your	? Bruder	? Schwester
his	? Bruder	? Schwester
her	? Bruder	? Schwester
no	? Bruder	? Schwester

Look back at the letter and photo opposite and describe Christel's family. Use the words in the box to complete the text:

1 Christel ist ____ Jahre alt.
2 Ihr ____ heißt Georg.
3 ____ Mutter heißt Verena.
4 Ihr Bruder Paul ist ____ Jahre alt.
5 ____ Bruder Volker ist acht.
6 ____ Vater ist ____.
7 Ihre Mutter ist ____.
8 ____ hat keine Schwester.

```
einundvierzig
ihr
ihr
ihre
sie
Vater
vierzig
zehn
zwölf
```

Konversationen

Claudia: Wie heißt dein Bruder, Elke?
Elke: Mein Bruder? Er heißt Rainer.
Claudia: Und wie alt ist er?
Elke: Fünfzehn.

Bernd: Wie heißt deine Schwester, Axel?
Axel: Meine Schwester? Sie heißt Manuela.
Bernd: Und wie alt ist sie?
Axel: Dreizehn.

Und jetzt du!

Ask the name and age of your friend's brother and sister. If you do not have any, make them up!

Geschwister

Ich habe   einen Bruder   drei Brüder   eine Schwester   vier Schwestern

✱ Kapiert?

Fill in the chart to show how many brothers and sisters each person has and how old they are.

	Brüder?		Schwestern?	
	Wieviele?	Wie alt?	Wieviele?	Wie alt?
Volker				
Daniela				
Doris				
Michael				
Renate				

ℹ

Was?	Wie?
ask if someone has any brothers or sisters	Hast du Geschwister?
answer	Ja. Nein, keine.
find out how many	Wieviele?
answer	Ich habe einen Bruder. zwei Brüder. eine Schwester. zwei Schwestern. keine Geschwister. Ich bin Einzelkind.

🗣 Und jetzt du!

A: du bist Daniela.

1 Ask if Volker has any brothers or sisters.

3 Ask how many.

5 Ask how old they are.

B: du bist Volker.

2 Answer yes or no (refer to the grid you filled in for **Kapiert**).

4 Tell her how many brothers and how many sisters.

6 Tell her.

Andere Verwandte

Das ist mein Onkel.
Er heißt Friedrich.
Er ist 38 und er
wohnt in Hameln.
Das ist in Norddeutschland.

Hier ist Opa, Vatis Vater.
Er ist 69 und er wohnt
bei uns.

Das hier sind mein Cousin,
Ralf, und sein Freund.
Onkel Friedrich ist sein Vater.
Seine Mutter ist meine Tante
Ilse.
Ralf ist elf Jahre alt.

All these relatives are male. Here is how to talk about them. The word for 'he' is **er** in German.

Was?	Wie?		
Find out:			
– his name	Wie heißt	dein Vater / er	?
– his age	Wie alt ist	dein Bruder / er	?
– where he lives	Wo wohnt	dein Freund / er	?

Wie alt ist dein Bruder?

Was?	Wie?	
Give:		
– his name	Mein Vater / Er	heißt Karl.
– his age	Mein Bruder / Er	ist 15.
– where he lives	Mein Freund / Er	wohnt in Mainz.

Er ist 15.

Kannst du zeichnen?

Make a rough drawing of any male member of your family. Look at the drawing your partner has made and ask:

- who it is (**Wer ist das?**).
- what his name is.
- how old he is.
- where he lives.

Answer your partner's questions.

Das ist mein Onkel.
Er heißt Frankfurter.
Er wohnt in Hessen.
Er ist zwei Jahre alt.

Kannst du mehr? (Can you do more?)

Next to your drawing, write at least four statements in German about your relative. You may get ideas from the examples on the previous page. When you have done this, draw and describe some other male relatives or friends. The word for friend is **Freund**.

Mehr Verwandte

Hier sind meine Tante Ilse und meine Cousine, Svenja. Svenja ist natürlich Ralfs Schwester. Sie ist 13 Jahre alt. Tante Ilse ist 37. Sie wohnen natürlich in Hameln, mit Onkel Friedrich.

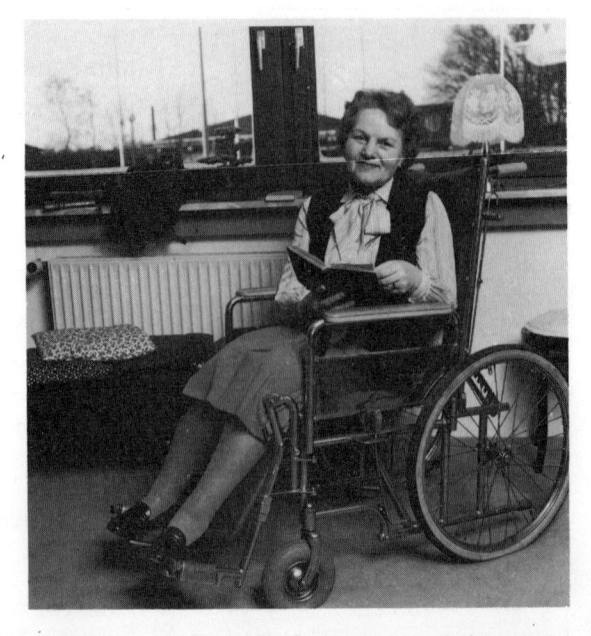

Das hier ist meine Oma, Muttis Mutter. Sie wohnt in Basel, in der Schweiz. Sie ist 67 Jahre alt. Ihr Mann, mein Opa, ist schon tot. Sie hat einen Rollstuhl.

These relatives are all female. This is how you talk about them. The word for 'she' ist **sie**.

Was?	Wie?
Find out:	
– her name	Wie heißt deine Mutter / sie ?
– her age	Wie alt ist deine Oma / sie ?
– where she lives	Wo wohnt deine Tante / sie ?

Wo wohnt deine Tante?

Was?	Wie?
Give	
– her name	Meine Mutter / Sie heißt Ute.
– her age	Meine Oma / Sie ist 48 Jahre alt.
– where she lives	Meine Tante / Sie wohnt in Ulm.

Sie wohnt in Ulm.

You will often need to talk about more than just one person. This is how to talk about several people. The word for 'they' is also **sie**. Can you spot the difference in German between 'What's her name?' and 'What are their names?'

Was?	Wie?	Was?	Wie?
Find out:		Give:	
– their names	Wie heißen sie?	– their names	Sie heißen Inge und Felix.
– their ages	Wie alt sind sie?	– their ages	Sie sind 16 und 9.
– where they live	Wo wohnen sie?	– where they live	Sie wohnen in Frankfurt.

Schon wieder zeichnen! (Drawing again!)

Draw a female relative and answer your partner's questions about her. Look at the questions on page 34.

Next, draw two or more friends or relatives who live in the same place. Again, ask and answer questions about them.

13   Das Jahr in Deutschland   13

Januar
Februar
März
April
Mai
Juni
Juli
August
September
Oktober
November
Dezember

Das Jahr hat zwölf Monate.

Im Januar ist es kalt. Da kann man skilaufen und Schlittenfahren.

Im Februar ist Fasching oder Karneval in Deutschland.

Ostern ist im März oder im April. Da kommt der Osterhase und es gibt Ostereier.

Im Mai wird es warm. Am ersten Mai ist Maifest. Da gibt es einen Maibaum.

Im Juni ist oft Pfingsten.

Sommerferien sind im Juli und im August.

Die Schule beginnt wieder im September.

Im Oktober wird es kalt.

Der November ist sehr grau und langweilig.

Im Dezember ist viel los. Am sechsten Dezember kommt der Nikolaus. Am 24 Dezember ist Weihnachten und am einunddreißigsten ist Sylvester. Dann ist das Jahr zu Ende.

Ask your teacher to explain some of the German customs to you. Then answer the following questions in English.

Antworte auf englisch

1 What takes place in February?
2 In which months can Easter be?
3 When is Whitsuntide?
4 When does school start again in Germany?
5 Which three things are mentioned about December?

Die Tage
Montag
Dienstag
Mittwoch
Donnerstag
Freitag
Samstag
Sonntag

Kannst du mehr?

Dann antworte auf deutsch:

1 Wann ist Karneval?
2 Wann ist Ostern?
3 Wann ist Pfingsten?
4 Wann gibt's Sommerferien?
5 Wann kommt der Nikolaus?

Den wievielten haben wir heute?

1 der erste
2 der zweite
3 der dritte
4 der vierte
5 der fünfte
6 der sechste
7 der siebte
8 der achte
9 der neunte
10 der zehnte

This is how you count in German from 'the first' to 'the tenth'. What are always the last two letters?

Und jetzt du!

These boys are just finishing the 800 metres race. Tell your partner what order they are in. Partner **A** takes the odd numbers, **B** takes the even numbers.

Beispiel: Karl ist der erste.

Gehirnarbeit (Brainwork)

To form the words for 11th to 19th, you just put **–te** on the end of each number. Say them and write them out.

Was?	Wie?
ask for today's date	Den wievielten haben wir heute?
give today's date	Heute ist Freitag, der dreizehnte April.

Und jetzt du!

Give these dates in full, as in the information box, when your partner asks you. Take turns to ask and answer.

1 Mo 1. Jan.
2 So 12. Feb.
3 Mi 12. Juli
4 Fr 15. Apr.
5 Do 8. Nov.
6 Di 3. Okt.
7 Sa 6. März
8 Mo 2. Mai
9 Fr 4. Dez.
10 Mi 19. Aug.
11 So 7. Juni
12 Di 5. Sep.

Wann hast du Geburtstag?

Kais Geburtstag ist heute, der vierzehnte Mai. Er ist dreizehn Jahre alt. Er feiert eine Party mit seinen Freunden.

Was?	Wie?
ask when a friend's birthday is	Wann hast du Geburtstag?
answer	Mein Geburtstag ist der 14. Mai.

Gehirnarbeit

To form the words for 20th onwards, you add **–ste** to the numbers.

Beispiele: 20. der zwanzigste
21. der einundzwanzigste
30. der dreißigste

Count from 1st onwards as far as you can in three minutes. Then work out how to give your birthday in German.

Kapiert?

Tick the correct box to show whose birthday it is.

	Carsten	Kai	Silke	Markus	Bettina
der 2. Feb.					
der 14. Mai					
der 28. Dez.					
der 8. Aug.					
der 12. Dez.					

Und jetzt du!

Write out a questionnaire with the following questions in German:

- what's your name?
- where do you come from?
- how old are you?
- when is your birthday?
- have you any brothers or sisters?

Ask five of your classmates to answer your questions.

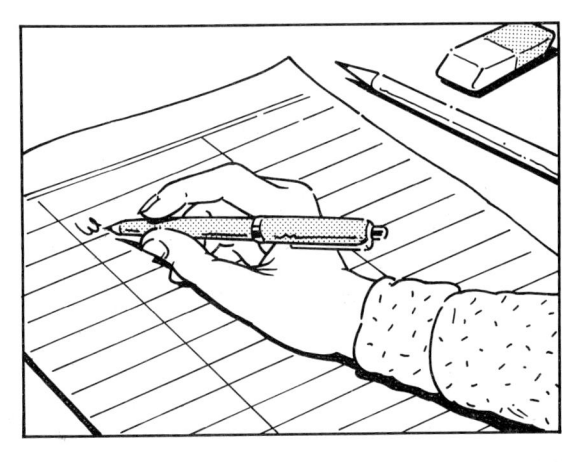

14 Wie bitte? 14

Das Alphabet
A B C D E F G
H I J K L M N O P
Q R S T U V W X Y Z

Das ist anders:
(This is different)
ä ö ü ß

Kannst du das laut lesen?
(Can you read these aloud?)

Kapiert?

1 Who does the caller want to speak to, the doctor or his receptionist?
2 Spell the caller's name.
3 Why is the caller not successful?

Und noch mehr (And some more)

Three people are going to give you important information. Write down what they spell for you.

Und jetzt du!

Imagine you are giving your name and address to a German who understands no English. Spell them in German. Do the same with a made-up name and address. Ask your partner to write down what you say. Did he or she get it right? If not, why not? Did you spell everything correctly? Did you speak clearly?

Verstehst du das?

Sometimes we could understand a lot more if people would only speak more slowly or louder or if they would just repeat what they said. To get this message across is very important, no matter which language you speak.

Here is how to do it in German.

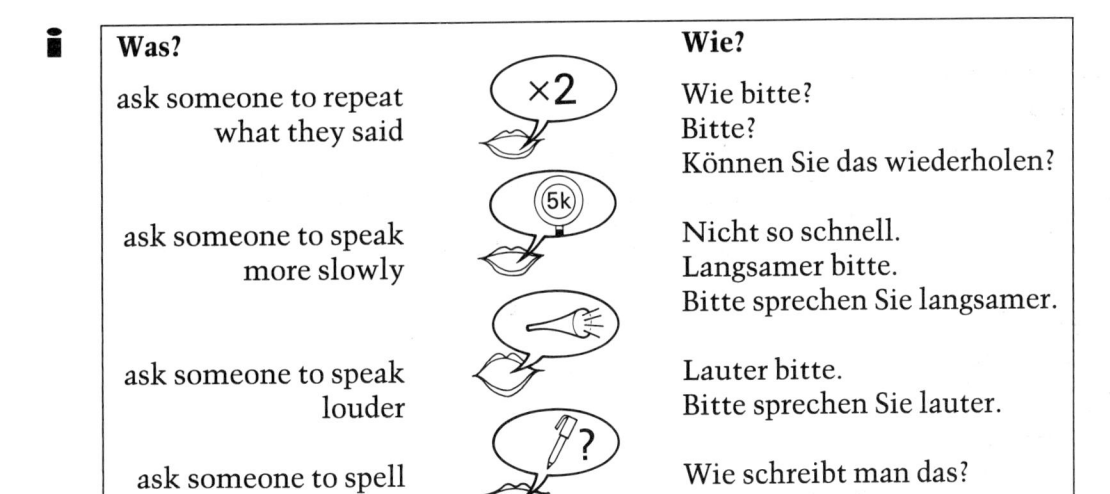

Was?		Wie?
ask someone to repeat what they said		Wie bitte? Bitte? Können Sie das wiederholen?
ask someone to speak more slowly		Nicht so schnell. Langsamer bitte. Bitte sprechen Sie langsamer.
ask someone to speak louder		Lauter bitte. Bitte sprechen Sie lauter.
ask someone to spell something		Wie schreibt man das? Bitte buchstabieren.

Kapiert?

These Germans are asking for clarification as they did not understand the first time. Copy the grid, then write the number of each sentence in the correct square. If you think the first speaker asks you to repeat what has been said, write a **1** in the first square, next to 'repeat'. You will hear 12 requests, so each square should be filled.

Repeat			
Spell			
Speak up			
Slow down			

It also helps if you can ask how to say something in English or German. Here's how to do so.

Was?		Wie?
ask what something is in English		Wie heißt das auf englisch?
ask what something is in German		Wie heißt das auf deutsch?

Wiederholung Drei

Kapiert?

Antworte auf englisch:

1. Is Svenja German?
2. Does Lao still live in Vietnam?
3. How old is Sandra?
4. What is the name of Thorsten's little brother?
5. Who is in the photograph?
6. When is Marco's birthday?
7. When is Jutta's birthday?
8. Where does the boy's aunt live?
9. What does the girl want you to do?
10. What does the boy want you to do?

Hamburg, den 20. Januar

Lieber Rainer,

Hallo! Wie geht's? Uns geht es gut.
Hier ist ein Foto von meiner Familie bei Opas Geburtstagsfest. Er ist jetzt fünfundsechzig Jahre alt. Sein Geburtstag ist der vierte Januar. Auf dem Foto sind mein Opa und meine Oma, mein Vater, meine Schwester, meine Mutter und ihre Schwester, Tante Petra. Meine Schwester heißt Pia und sie ist sieben Jahre alt.

Ich bin nicht auf dem Foto.

Sende mir ein Foto von Dir und Deiner Familie, bitte.

Viele Grüße
Dein
Achim.

Antworte auf englisch

1. Who wrote this letter?
2. Where does he live?
3. Whose family is in the photo?
4. How old is his grandfather?
5. What month is his grandfather's birthday.
6. How old is his sister Pia?

Kannst du mehr?

Antworte auf deutsch:

1. Wo ist Achim, in Hamburg oder in Hameln?
2. Ist das Foto von seiner Familie?
3. Wie alt ist sein Opa?
4. Wann ist sein Geburtstag?
5. Wie heißt Achims Schwester?
6. Ist Achim auf dem Foto?

NOW YOU ARE READY FOR WAYSTAGE 3.

15 — Deutsches Geld — 15

Deutsches Geld heißt **Mark**. Eine Mark hat 100 **Pfennig**.

Hier sind die Münzen:

ein Pfennig	fünf Pfennig	zehn Pfennig	fünfzig Pfennig	eine Mark
1 Pf	5 Pf	10 Pf	50 Pf	1 DM

zwei Mark 2 DM    fünf Mark 5 DM    zehn Mark 10 DM   zwanzig Mark 20 DM

Hier sind die Banknoten:

zehn Mark 10 DM

zwanzig Mark 20 DM

fünfzig Mark 50 DM

hundert Mark 100 DM

fünfhundert Mark 500 DM

tausend Mark 1000 DM

Problem solving

Wieviel Mark bekommst du für ein Pfund?
How many marks do you get for £1?

Look in your daily paper to find out the bank rate. If you had each of the above banknotes, how much money would you get for each one?

⊛ Kapiert?

Listen to the tape and find out which German coins and banknotes are mentioned. Make a list in your exercise book.

Was?	Wie?
ask how much something costs	Was kostet das?
ask how much something is in English money	Was kostet das in englischem Geld?
say something is too expensive	Das ist zu teuer.
say something is cheap	Das ist aber billig.

Was kostet das?

Hier sind verschiedene Sachen:

(Pullover DM 99, Bleistift DM 0,30, Tasche DM 49,90, Krawatte DM 17,50, Schuhe DM 120,50, Radiergummi DM 0,70, Spitzer DM 0,95, Lineal DM 1,20)

⊛ Hör gut zu! Richtig oder falsch?

Look at the pictures above. Read the following statements as you listen to the tape and decide whether they are true or false. Write **R** for **Richtig**, **F** for **Falsch**.

1. Ein Radiergummi kostet siebzig Pfennig.
2. Ein Pullover kostet neunzig Mark.
3. Ein Bleistift kostet eine Mark zwanzig.
4. Ein Paar Schuhe kostet hundertzwanzig Mark fünfzig.
5. Ein Lineal kostet eine Mark zwanzig.
6. Ein Spitzer kostet fünfundneunzig Pfennig.
7. Eine Tasche kostet neunundvierzig Mark fünfzig.
8. Eine Krawatte kostet siebzehn Mark fünfzig.

What coins or notes do you need to pay for each item?
Beispiel: 70 Pfennig = 2 × 10 Pfennig
+
1 × 50 Pfennig

Wieviel ist das in englischem Geld?

Rechnen (Sums)

Look at the prices of the items shown on page 44 opposite. You have to work out how much each item costs (more or less) in English money. Use the bankrate you found in the paper, or ask your teacher how much one Mark is worth at the moment.

List your answers like this:
   ein Radiergummi = DM 0.70 = X pence

A useful word is '**ungefähr**'. It means 'more or less'.

Was kostet das in England?

What would you expect to pay for each of the items on page 44? Make sentences like this:

   Ein Radiergummi kostet 10 pence in England.

(Remember, Germans often refer to the whole of Great Britain as 'England'.)

Ist das billig oder teuer in Deutschland?

Use the information you have collected so far to compare prices in Britain and Germany. Make statements like this:
   Ein Radiergummi kostet 10 pence in England.
   Ein Radiergummi kostet DM 0,70 (20 pence) in Deutschland.
   Das ist teuer.

Make three statements about the price of each item opposite.

🗣 Und jetzt du!

Partner **A** ist Verkäufer. Partner **B** kauft ein.
A is the salesperson. *B is doing the shopping.*

Hier sind deine Waren. Erfindet Dialoge.
Here is your stock. How many different dialogues can you make up?

Du:	Guten Tag.
Dein Partner:	Guten Tag. Was kostet ein Pullover?
Du:	Fünfzig Mark.
Dein Partner:	Das ist zu teuer.

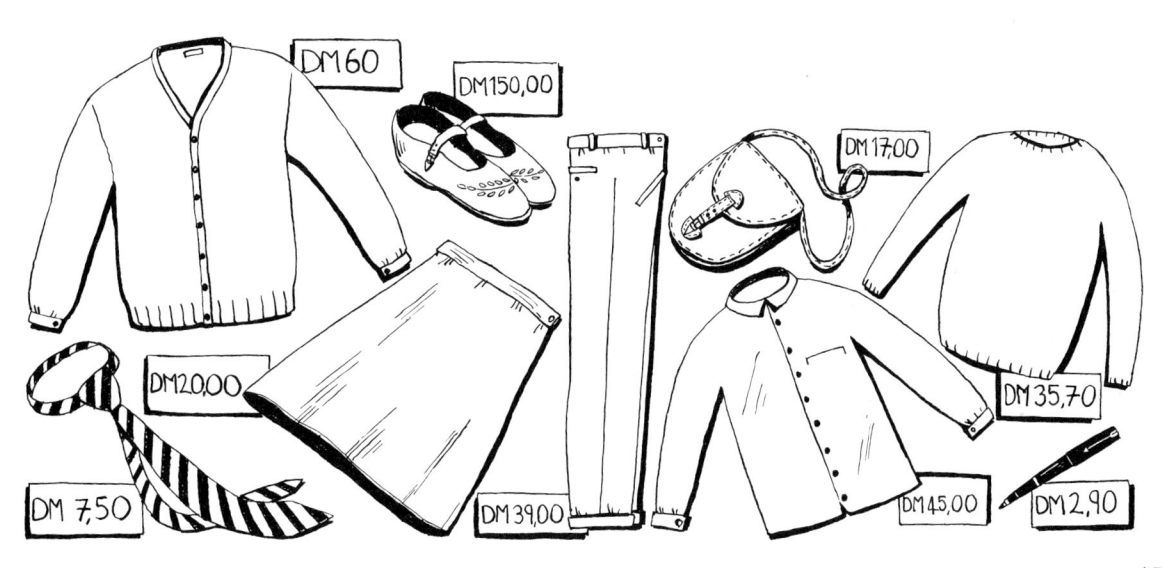

DM 60
DM 150,00
DM 17,00
DM 20,00
DM 35,70
DM 7,50
DM 39,00
DM 45,00
DM 2,90

16 — In der Imbißstube — 16

Das sind die Behälter:

eine Flasche zwei Flaschen eine Tasse zwei Tassen

ein Kännchen ein Glas ein Teller ein Stück

Was gibt's zu essen?

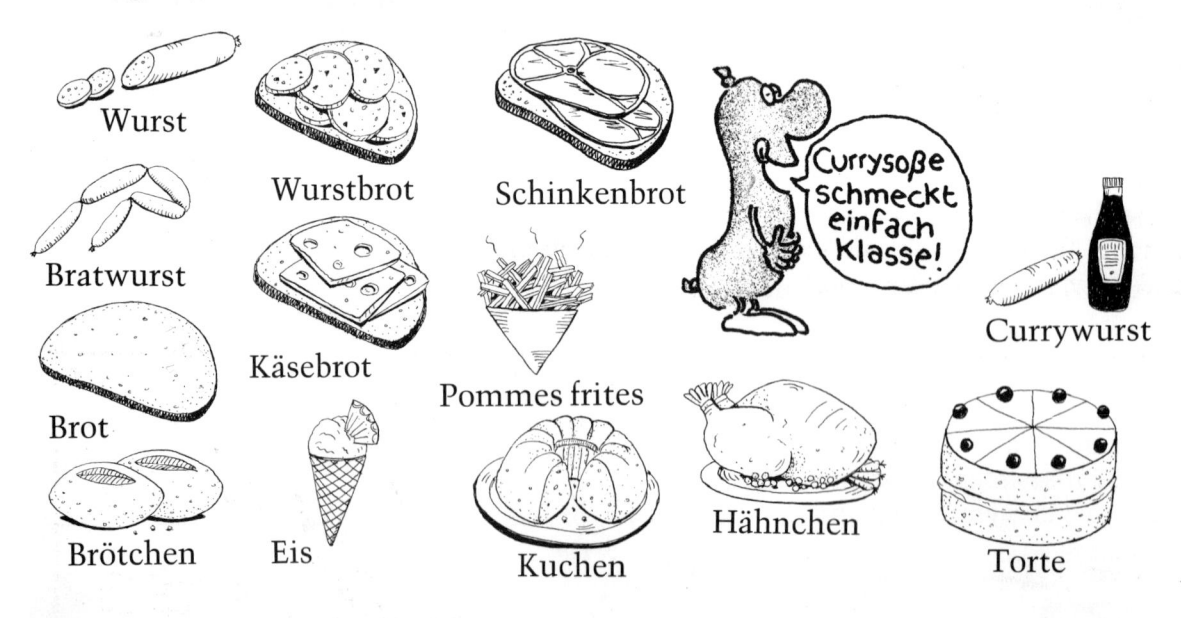

Wurst Wurstbrot Schinkenbrot

Bratwurst Käsebrot Pommes frites Currywurst

Currysoße schmeckt einfach Klasse!

Brot Eis Kuchen Hähnchen Torte

Brötchen

Was gibt's zu trinken?

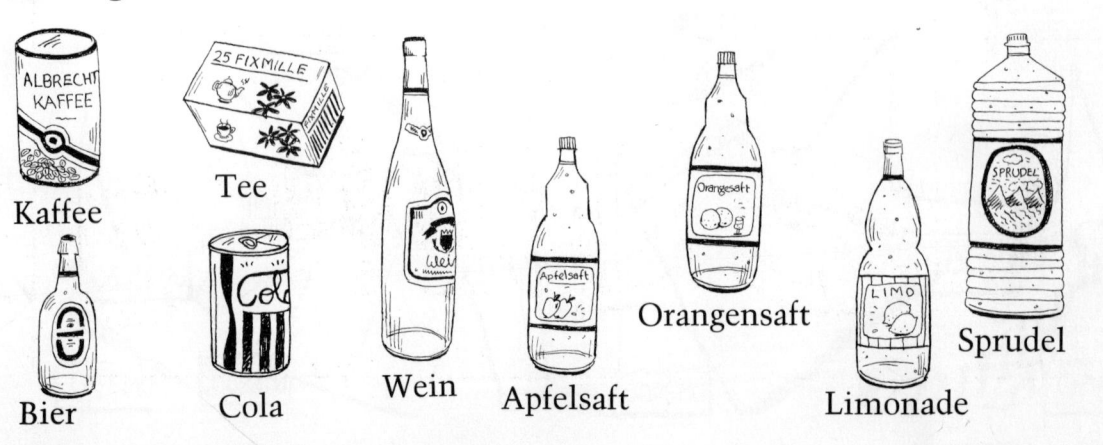

Kaffee Tee Wein Apfelsaft Orangensaft Limonade Sprudel

Bier Cola

46

	Was?	**Wie?**
	ask what something is	Was ist das?
	ask what it costs	Was kostet das?
	ask what there is to eat	Was gibt's hier zu essen?
		Was kann man hier essen?
	ask what there is to drink	Was gibt's hier zu trinken?
		Was kann man hier trinken?
	ask if they have something	Haben Sie …?
	say 'of course'	Aber sicher.
		Ja, natürlich.
	say 'no, sorry'	Nein, tut mir leid.
	ask how something tastes	Wie schmeckt's?
	answer	Gut!
		Einfach Klasse!

Kapiert?

Hör zu!
Hier sind zehn Konversationen. Welche Konversation paßt zu welchem Bild?
Match the conversations you hear to the pictures below. Write the number of the conversation and the letter of the picture in your exercise book. You should end up with a delicious word!

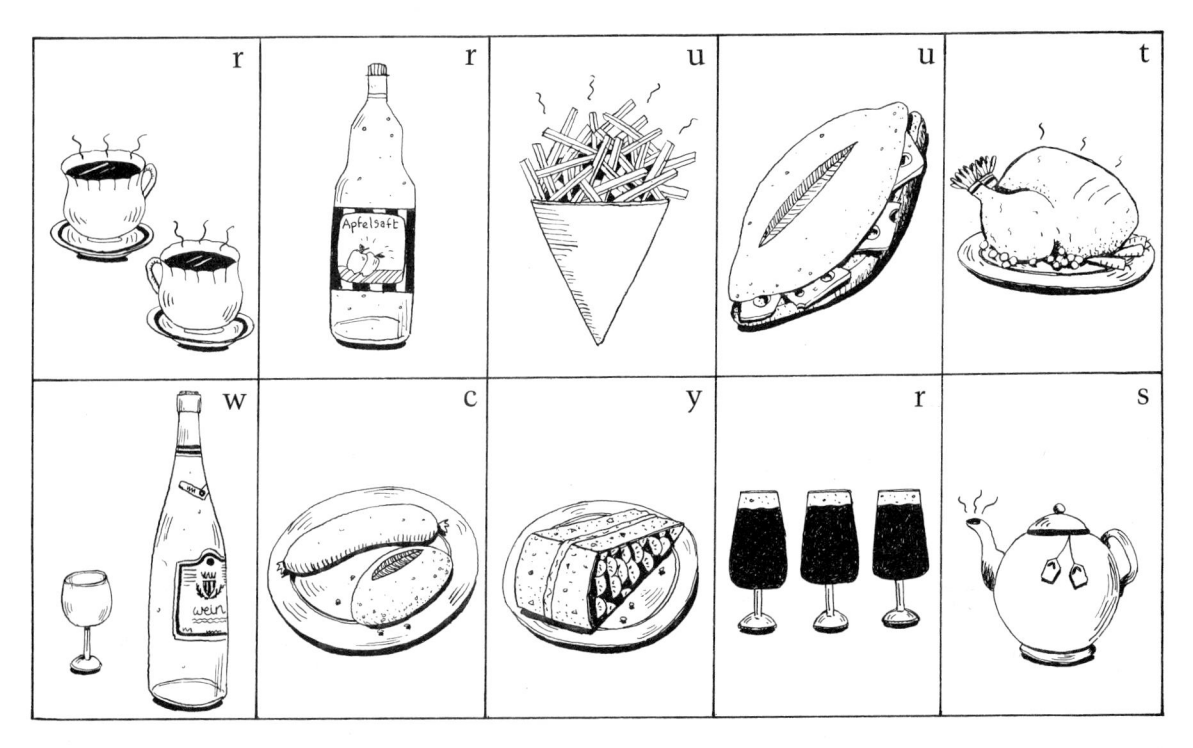

r	r	u	u	t
w	c	y	r	s

47

Kaffeeklatsch

Using the pictures on page 46, see how many dialogues you can work out with your partner. There is an example on the tape.
Hör gut zu!

A: Guten Tag. Was ist das?

B: Das? Currywurst mit Brötchen.

A: Ah! Was kostet das?

B: Zwei Mark fünfzig.

A: Danke.

Ask your partner:
– what different things are.
– what it costs.

Tell your partner:
– the name of the thing he or she points to.
– the price of the item he or she points to.

Here are examples for different dialogues:

A: Guten Tag. Was haben Sie zu essen?
B: Bratwurst, Hähnchen, Currywurst.
A: Was kostet eine Bratwurst?
B: Drei Mark bitte.
A: Bitte, eine Bratwurst.

A: Guten Tag. Haben Sie Käsebrot?
B: Nein, tut mir leid.
A: Was haben Sie zu essen?
B: Wurstbrot, Schinkenbrot, Currywurst.
A: Was kostet ein Schinkenbrot?
B: Vier Mark.
A: Ja, gut. Ein Schinkenbrot bitte.
B: Bitte. Auf Wiedersehen.
A: Auf Wiedersehen.

Kannst du mehr?

Imagine you have a holiday job in a café. A German tourist (your partner) comes in. Try to have a conversation. See if you can keep talking German for three minutes!

Ein Bilderrätsel
Was ist denn das?

Eine Tasse
Ein Glas
Ein Teller

Eine Flasche Wein
Eine Flasche Bier
Ein Kännchen Kaffee

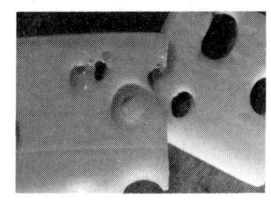

Ein Stück Käse
Ein Stück Kuchen
Ein Stück Wurst

Ein Glas Bier
Eine Tasse Kaffee
Eine Flasche Limo

EINS A IMBISS

SPEISEN		GETRÄNKE	
Belegte Brote:		Tasse Kaffee	DM 1,80
Käsebrot	DM 3,50	Tasse Tee	DM 1,80
Wurstbrot	DM 3,75	Glas Cola/Limo	DM 1,50
Schinkenbrot	DM 4,00	Glas Apfelsaft	DM 2,00
Bratwurst mit Brötchen	DM 2,80	Glas Orangensaft	DM 2,00
Currywurst mit Pommes frites	DM 3,10	Flasche Bier 0,3 l	DM 1,50
½ Hähnchen mit Brot	DM 4,50	Glas Wein 0,25 l	DM 2,50
1 Portion Pommes frites	DM 1,50		
1 Stück Kuchen	DM 1,80		
Eis	DM 1,20		

Gehirnarbeit

You are in a German town with your friend. Between you you have 10 DM. You both are quite hungry and thirsty. How would you spend your money?

Choose a snack and a drink each and write what you would buy in your exercise book. How much money would you have left?

Noch ein Rätsel

Copy the spiral and write in the German names of the items. The last letter of one word is the first letter of the next.

17 Essen in Deutschland 17

Die Zeiten	*Times*
morgens / vormittags	in the morning
mittags	at lunchtime
nachmittags	in the afternoon
abends	in the evening
nachts	at night

Frühstück
Morgens — zwischen 6 und 8 Uhr — zu Hause

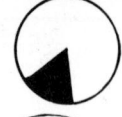

Kaffee 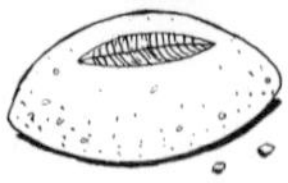   Brötchen    Butter    Marmelade    Wurst    Käse    ein Ei

Zweites Frühstück
Vormittags — zwischen 10 und 11 Uhr — in der Schule / in der Fabrik / im Büro

Apfel   Trauben   Käsebrot   Wurstbrot   Kaffee   Milch
Banane   Pfirsich   Schinkenbrot   Limo

Mittagessen
Mittags — zwischen 12 und 2 Uhr — zu Hause / in der Kantine

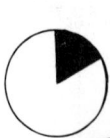

Suppe    Fleisch    Soße   Kartoffeln   Salat
Wein   Bier   Sprudel     Limo   Saft    Gemüse 

50

Kaffee und Kuchen
Nachmittags    zwischen 3 und 4 Uhr | zu Hause
                                           | im Café

Kaffee    Kuchen 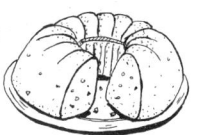   Torte

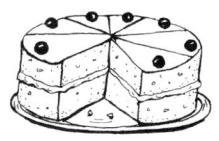

Abendessen
Abends    zwischen 6 und 8 Uhr   zu Hause

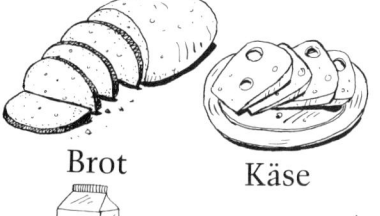

Brot   Käse    Schinken    Wurst    Butter    Salat

Milch    Tee    Kakao     Sprudel    Saft   Limo     Wein    Bier

Was?			Wie?		
ask what time	breakfast elevenses lunch coffee and cake the evening meal	is	Wann gibt es	Frühstück zweites Frühstück Mittagessen Kaffee und Kuchen Abendessen	?
ask what there is for	breakfast lunch the evening meal		Was gibt es zum	Frühstück Mittagessen Abendessen	?
ask what you drink with your lunch			Was trinkt man zum Mittagessen?		

Kapiert?

This is an inverview with Susanne about the mealtimes of her family. Write in your exercise book when she has her meals, and, if you can, anything else she says about them.

Was gehört zusammen?

Test your knowledge of German meals. Match the food and drink in the column on the right with the names of the meals in the column on the left.

Frühstück	Sprudel, Suppe, Fleisch, Gemüse
Zweites Frühstück	Kaffee, Torte
Mittagessen	Kaffee, Brötchen, Ei, Marmelade
Kaffee und Kuchen	Tee, Brot, Wurst, Käse, Salat
Abendessen	Milch, belegte Brote

Wer ißt was zum Mittagessen?

Find out what each of the people below has for lunch. Schreibe die Antworten in dein Heft.

Hans ißt _____ und _____ und _____.

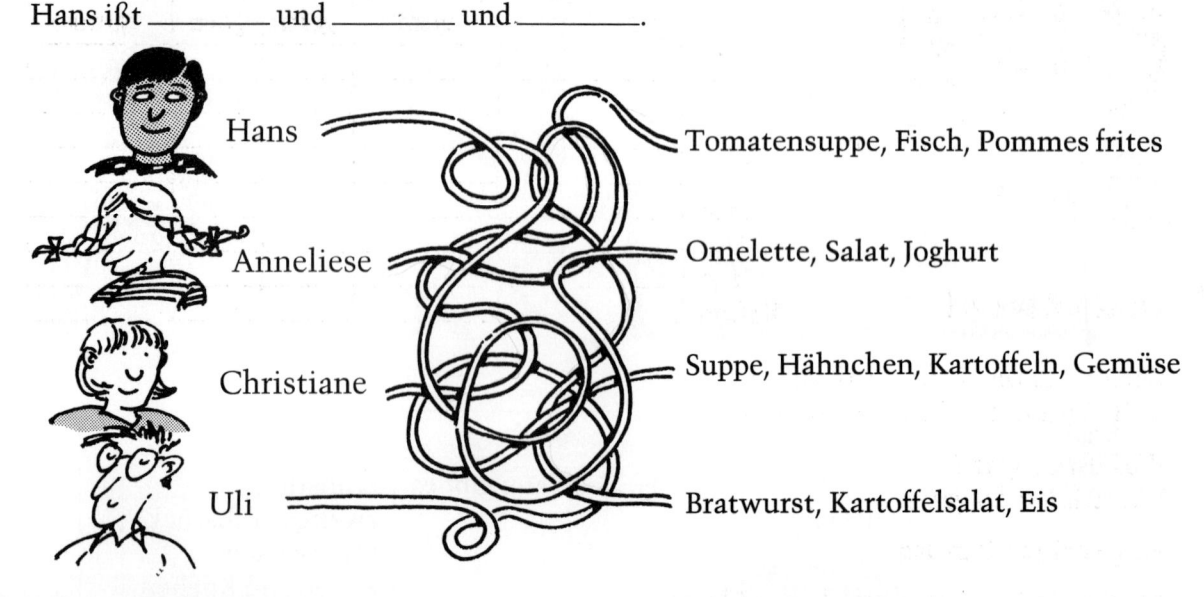

Hans — Tomatensuppe, Fisch, Pommes frites

Anneliese — Omelette, Salat, Joghurt

Christiane — Suppe, Hähnchen, Kartoffeln, Gemüse

Uli — Bratwurst, Kartoffelsalat, Eis

Kannst du mehr?

Antworte auf deutsch:

1 Wann ißt du Frühstück?
2 Wann ißt du zweites Frühstück?
3 Wann gibt's Mittagessen?
4 Gibt es in deiner Familie Kaffee und Kuchen?
5 Wann gibt es Abendessen?

Frage deinen Partner.

18   Was ißt du gern?   18

Was?	Wie?
ask what someone likes eating	Was ißt du gern?
	Was essen Sie gern?
ask what someone likes drinking	Was trinkst du gern?
	Was trinken Sie gern?
say what you love	Ich esse sehr gern Fleisch.
like	Ich trinke gern Milch.
quite like	Ich esse Kuchen ganz gern.
prefer	Ich trinke lieber Kaffee.
don't like	Ich esse nicht gern Schokolade.
hate	Ich trinke Whisky gar nicht gern.

Kapiert?

Two people are telling you what they think of certain foods and drinks. Copy the grid and note what they like and don't like.

Wolfgang   Ursel

	Wolfgang			Ursel		
	sehr gern	ganz gern	gar nicht gern	sehr gern	ganz gern	gar nicht gern
Fleisch						
Pfirsiche						
Pommes frites						
Kuchen						
Käsebrot						
Kaffee						
Tee						
Kakao						

Und jetzt du!

Look at all the different things to eat in units 16 and 17. What do *you* like?

Was ißt du gern?
Was trinkst du gern?

Frage deinen Partner.

Mache ein Interview mit deiner Klasse.

Name	sehr gern	ganz gern	gar nicht gern
Sonia	Eis	Schokolade	Salat

Und dein Lehrer oder deine Lehrerin? Was ißt er oder sie gern?
Was trinkt er oder sie gern?

53

19   Im Café/Restaurant   19

Was?	Wie?
call the waiter	Herr Ober!
call the waitress	Fräulein!
ask for the menu	Ich möchte bitte die Speisekarte.
ask if they have something	Haben Sie ein Käsebrot bitte?
order something	Ich möchte bitte eine Tasse Tee.
	Eine Portion Pommes frites bitte.
	Einmal Tomatensuppe bitte.
ask for the bill	Zahlen bitte!

What you may hear

Yes please.	Bitte schön?
Can I help you?	Bitte sehr?
What would you like?	Was darf's sein?
Anything else?	Sonst noch etwas?
That comes to 23 Marks.	Das macht 23 Mark.

What you may read

| menu | Speisekarte |
| Service and VAT included | Bedienung und Mehrwertsteuer inbegriffen |

Kapiert?

Hör zu!

Falsch oder richtig?

Decide which of the following statements is correct. Write **F** for **Falsch**, **R** for **Richtig**.

1 The customer calls a waiter.
2 The customer is on her own.
3 She would like some coffee.
4 The bill comes to 4,40 DM.

Was ist richtig?

Now look at the pairs of pictures below. Decide which of each pair is the correct one.

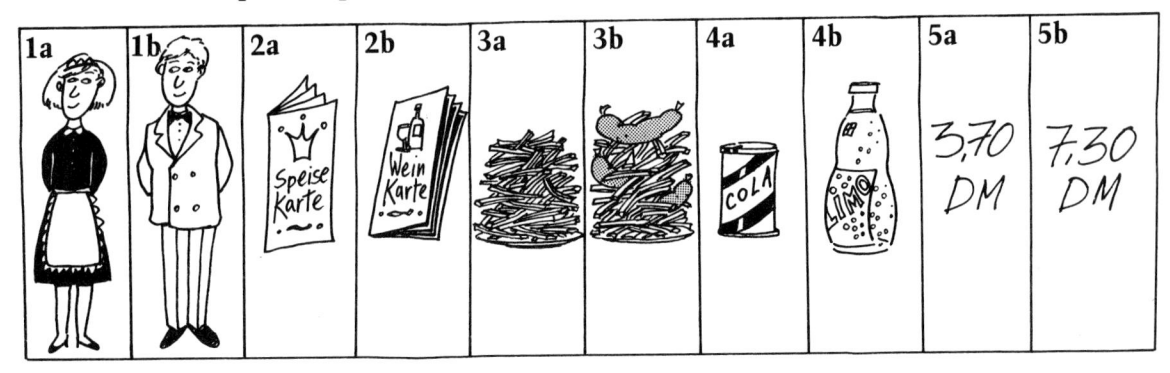

Ergänze

Complete the conversation so that it makes sense.

Kellner: Guten Tag. Bitte.
Kunde: Die ____ bitte.
Kellner: Bitte schön.
Kunde: ____ Sie Schinkenbrot?
Kellner: Ja sicher.
Kunde: ____ bitte und ____ Käsebrot.
Kellner: Sonst noch etwas?
Kunde: Ja, drei ____ Tee bitte.

Kunde: Herr Ober, ____ bitte!
Kellner: Zwei Schinkenbrot, ein Käsebrot und drei ____. Macht ____ Mark bitte.
Kunde: Bitte sehr.
Kellner: Danke. ____ Wiedersehen.

Das ist neu	
der Kellner	waiter
die Kellnerin	waitress
der Kunde	male customer
die Kundin	female customer

Kannst du mehr?

Make up your own café conversation, either in writing or with a partner.
Can you perfect your dialogue and act it out for the whole class?

55

🗨 Und jetzt du!

Look at the menu below. Together with your partner work out at least two dialogues with the two of you taking it in turns to be the waiter/waitress. Follow the instructions in number order.

A ist der Kellner/die Kellnerin.   **B** ist der Kunde/die Kundin.

1. Ask what the customer wants.
2. Ask for the menu.
3. Order something to eat or to drink.
4. Ask if the customer wants anything else.
5. Say that you want something/nothing else.
6. Bring the order.
7. Ask for the bill.
8. Tell the customer the price.
9. Pay, say thank you and goodbye.
10. Say thank you and goodbye.

CAFE MÜLLER

Kaffee		**Kuchen**	
Tasse	DM 2,10	Stück	DM 1,50
Kännchen	DM 4,—		
		Torte	
Tee		Stück	DM 2,20
Glas	DM 2,—		
Kännchen	DM 3,90	**Suppe**	
		Tasse	DM 2,50
Kakao			
Tasse	DM 2,50	**Wurstbrot**	DM 3,50
		Schinkenbrot	DM 3,50
Milch		**Käsebrot**	DM 3,00
0,2l Glas	DM —,90		
		Bratwurst mit	DM 4,00
Cola, Limo		**Pommes frites**	
0,2l Glas	DM 1,50		
		Hähnchen mit	DM 6,50
Sprudel		**Brot und Salat**	
0,3l Flasche	DM 1,20		
Wein			
0,25l Glas	DM 3,00		
Bier			
0,3l Flasche	DM 1,80		

Mehrwertsteuer und Bedienung sind in allen Preisen inbegriffen.

Wiederholung Vier

Kapiert?

What do these people want to eat and drink? Copy the grid, then fill in what each person buys and what he or she pays.

	Jörg	Birgit	Kai	Silke
Buys				
Pays				

Plappermaul

See how many conversations you can hold with your partner using this chart.

A = waiter
B = customer

A	Bitte sehr.	Was darf's sein?	Bitte schön?	Ja bitte?
B	Ich möchte ein Bier.	Eine Flasche Cola, bitte.	Ein Kännchen Kaffee.	Ein Glas Limo, bitte
A	Sonst noch etwas?	Und zu essen?	Möchten Sie etwas essen?	Sonst noch etwas?
B	Haben Sie Bratwurst?	Haben Sie Pommes frites?	Haben Sie Käsebrot?	Haben Sie Currywurst?
A	Ja, natürlich.	Aber sicher.	Nein, es tut mir leid.	Ja sicher.

Kannst du mehr?

Make your own 'Plappermaul' grid to help other British tourists work out conversations between a salesperson and a customer in a fashion boutique.

NOW YOU ARE READY FOR WAYSTAGE 4.

20 — In der Stadt — 20

Hallo! Ich heiße Lothar.
Ich bin 13 Jahre alt.
Ich komme aus Siegen.
Das ist in Westdeutschland.
Hier sind einige Fotos von Siegen.

Hier ist das Rathaus.

Hier ist das Schloß.

Und hier ist der Bahnhof.

Das ist die Post.

Das ist die Kirche.

Und das ist das Museum.

Hier ist die Fußgängerzone.

Und das ist der Marktplatz.

Das hier ist der Park.

Das ist das Verkehrsamt.

Hier ist das Sportzentrum.

Und das ist das Schwimmbad.

Und jetzt du!

Ask your partner to point out different photos.
A: Wo ist der Sportzentrum?

B: Hier. (*here*)
Dort drüben. (*over there*)

58

Kapiert?

Make a list of all the places in Siegen in German.
Then listen to the tape of a guided tour of the town.
Tick off all the places which are mentioned.
Listen again, and this time number the places in the order in which they are mentioned.
Finally write out the list in the correct order.

**Rate was das ist!
(Guess what this is!)**

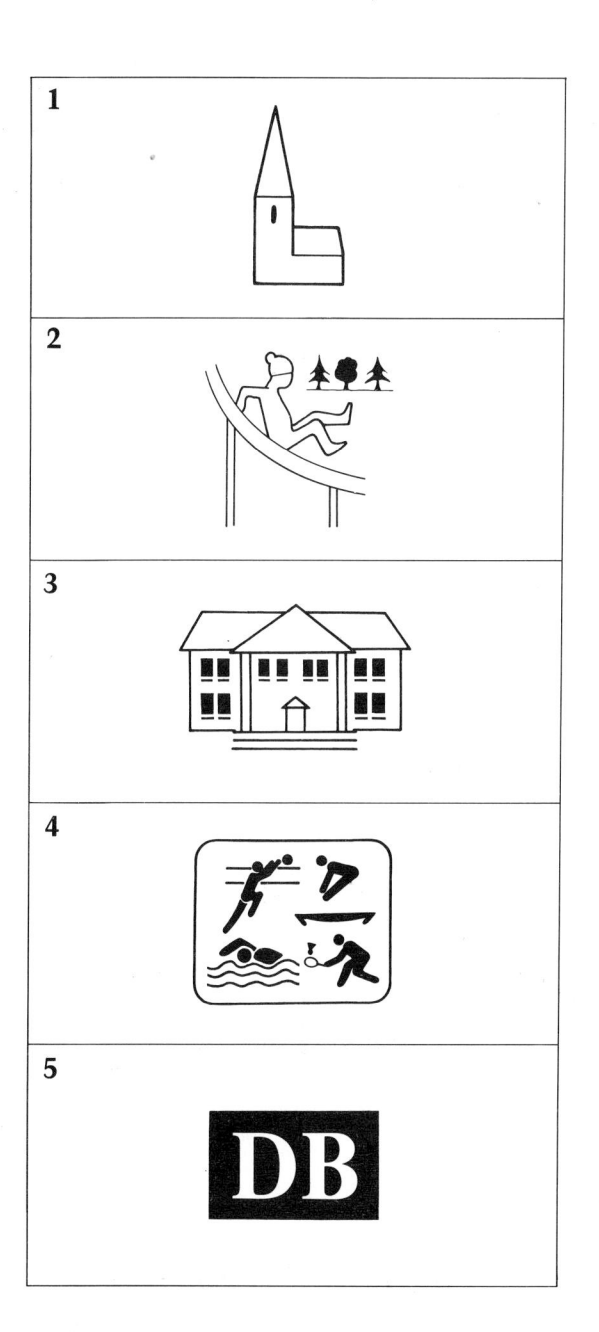

Beispiel:
Was ist Nummer eins?
—Die Kirche.

Stadtplan Siegen

Here is a plan of Siegen town centre. The buildings you know (and some you don't yet know) are marked, but symbols need to be drawn by the words to help foreign visitors. Copy the plan onto a full page in your book and draw in the symbols in the correct boxes. As you learn the names of more places in town, add them to the town plan. You will also need to use your plan for work on asking directions, so make sure it is carefully drawn and labelled.

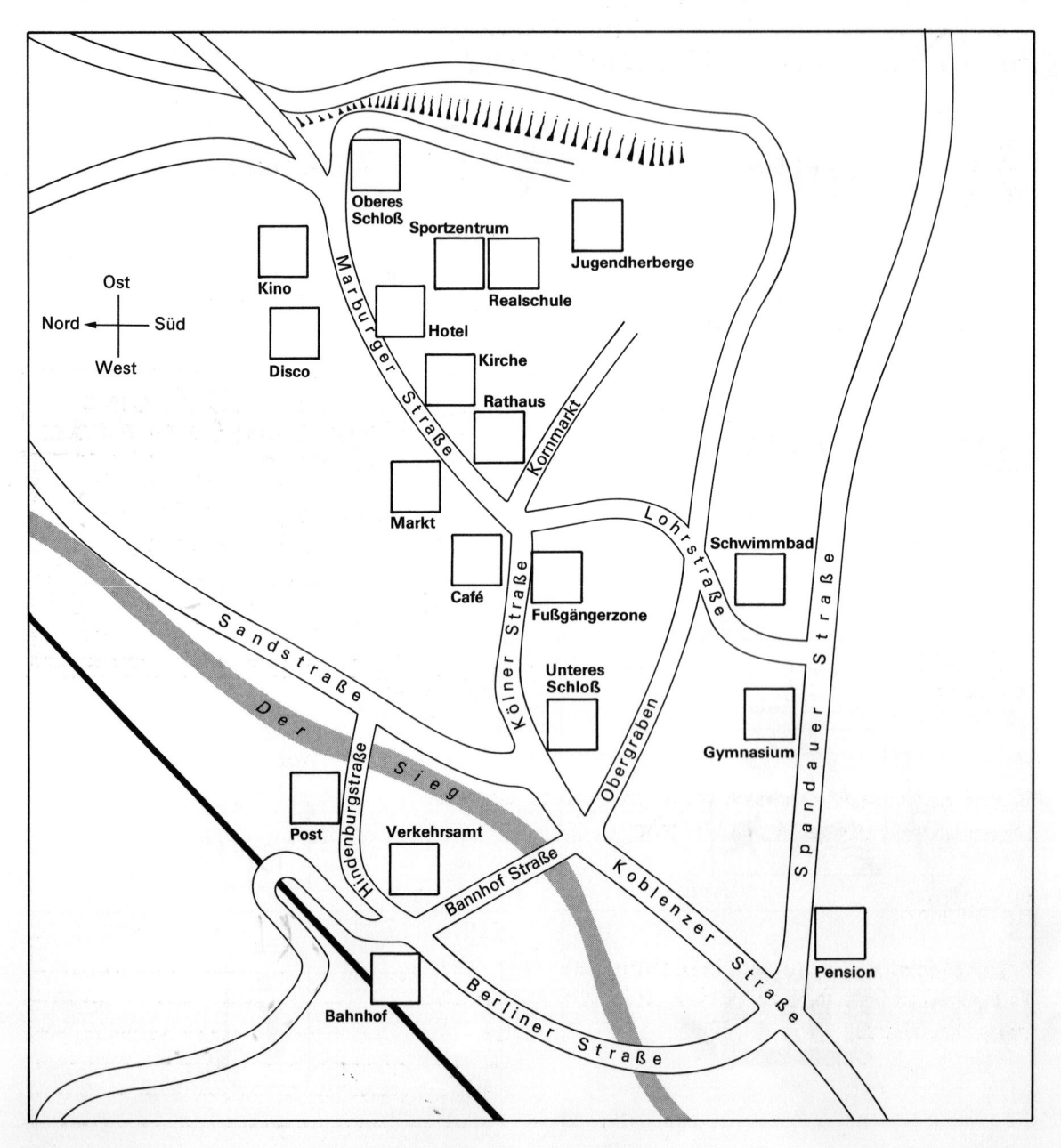

60

Ist hier eine Disco?

There may well be more than one station, park, or sports centre in a large town. If so, it will sound silly to ask for 'the' park or whatever you are looking for. If you are not sure if there is a particular place at all, say a disco, or if you think there may be several, ask:
Ist hier eine Disco?

> **ACHTUNG!**
> Do you remember how to check whether a noun is **der**, **die**, or **das**? Look in the back of the book!

Und jetzt du!

Ask your partner about the places listed. Answer by referring to the town plan with '**Ja, hier**' or '**Nein.**'

- ein Hotel 
- eine Pension (*bed & breakfast*) 
- Eine Jugendherberge (*youth hostel*) 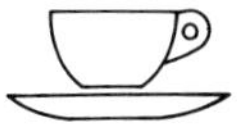
- ein Café 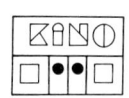
- ein Kino (*cinema*) 
- eine Disco 
- eine Toilette

iMBiSSSTUBE
Brat und Curry Wurstel

Hier wohne ich.

When you have both asked about each place, draw in the new symbols on your own map.

Kapiert?

What places are these people looking for? Put a grid in your book like this and fill it in as you listen.

Place
1 _____
2 _____
3 _____
4 _____
5 _____

21 Was ist denn das? 21

Look at the photos and at the clues. There are many words you have not met before. See if you can guess what each place is. Write out your answers like this:

1 Das ist ein Café.

1 Hier kannst du essen und trinken.

2 Und hier kannst du schwimmen.

3 Hier kannst du tanzen.

4 Hier kannst du einen Stadtplan bekommen.

5 Hier kannst du einen Markt sehen.

6 Und hier kannst du einen Film sehen.

7 Du kannst hier übernachten.

8 Du kannst hier Briefmarken bekommen.

Was?	Wie?
ask what something is	Was ist das?
ask what it is called in German	Wie heißt das auf deutsch?
ask where something is	Wo ist der Bahnhof?
	Wo ist das Museum?
	Wo ist die Burg?
say where something is	Hier.
	Dort drüben.

Und jetzt du!

A: Choose a photo. Ask what it is or what it is called in German, or ask where it is.

B: Answer your partner's questions.

Wo ist das genau?

| Das Kino ist neben der Diskothek. | Die Toilette ist neben dem Rathaus. | Die Post ist neben dem Bahnhof. |

Kapiert?

Listen to these strangers in town. Work out which buildings are next to which, and put a cross in the right box.

	neben der Burg	neben dem Rathaus	neben der Kirche	neben dem Bahnhof
1 die Toilette				
2 das Kino				
3 die Post				
4 das Museum				

Wo ist es?

Refer to the map on page 60. Complete these sentences correctly.

1 Die Disco ist neben dem K__.
2 Das Verkehrsamt ist neben dem B__.
3 Das Sportzentrum ist neben dem S__.
4 Die Kirche ist neben dem M__.
5 Das Schwimmbad ist neben dem G__.
6 Die Realschule ist neben der J__.
7 Der Marktplatz ist neben der K__.
8 Das Sportzentrum ist neben der R__.

Gewinnspiel

Copy the grid above twice. On one, put four crosses anywhere to show where buildings 1–4 are in your own imaginary town. Don't let your opponent see!

In pairs, play to win. In turn, ask in German where buildings 1–4 are:

A: Wo ist die Post?
B: Neben der Kirche?
A: Ja./Nein.

If your opponent guesses correctly, you cross off that building and do not ask about it again. The first to guess all four is the winner.

TIP
On your blank grid, fill in the information you have about your opponent's town.

Wo ist das schon wieder?

Here are some new words, called 'prepositions' because they tell you the exact position of things.

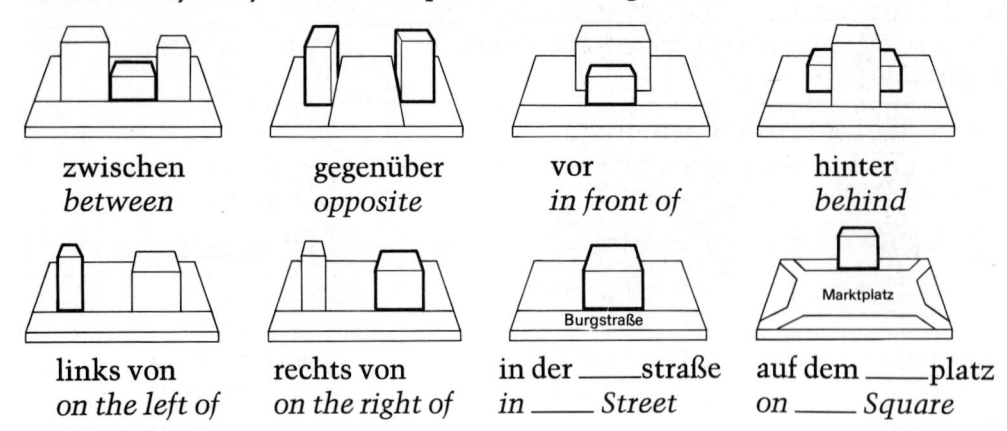

zwischen
between

gegenüber
opposite

vor
in front of

hinter
behind

links von
on the left of

rechts von
on the right of

in der ____straße
in ____ Street

auf dem ____platz
on ____ Square

Ergänze

Each drawing shows two buildings. Complete the sentences to say what they are. The first one is done for you.

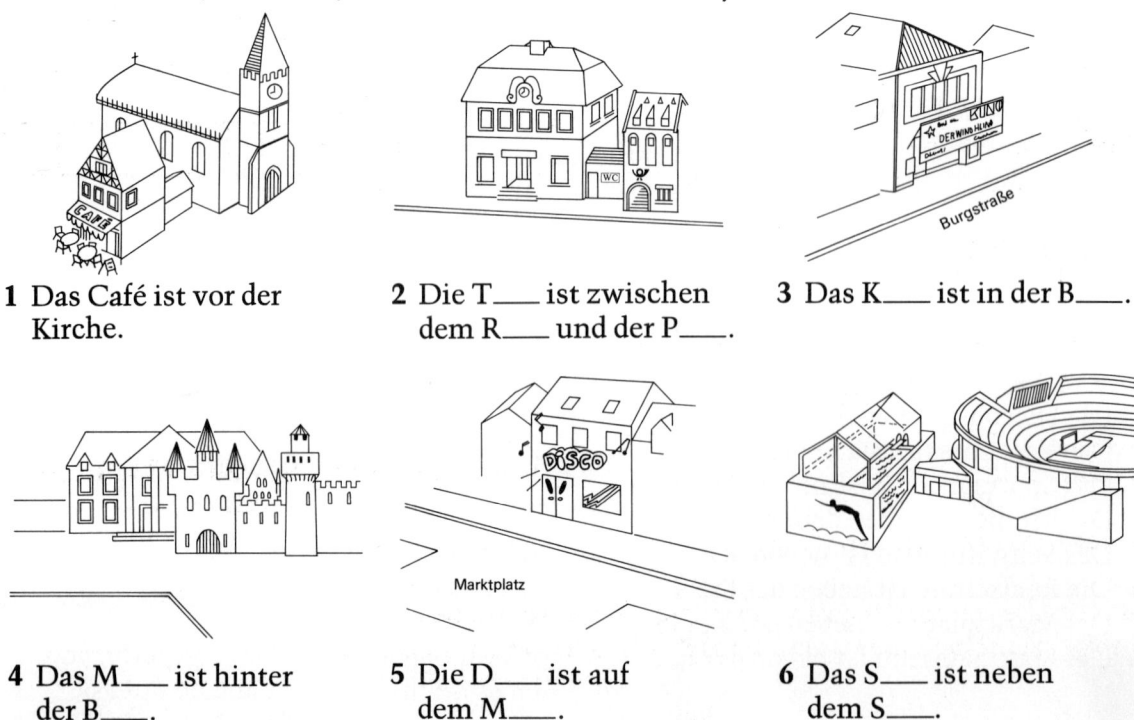

1 Das Café ist vor der Kirche.

2 Die T___ ist zwischen dem R___ und der P___.

3 Das K___ ist in der B___.

4 Das M___ ist hinter der B___.

5 Die D___ ist auf dem M___.

6 Das S___ ist neben dem S___.

Kannst du mehr?

Think about your own town. Could you explain to a German visitor where the important buildings are? You could act a scene out with your partner.

Kannst du Deutsch schreiben?

Write as many true sentences as you can in German about where buildings are on your own town plan. Try to make up at least three sentences about every building. You can say what it is next to, what it is near, what it is in front of, and so on.

Don't worry too much about whether every single word is perfectly correct. As long as a German could understand what you mean, that is good enough at the moment.

Kapiert?

Copy the grid.
Silke is telling you where places are in her town. As you listen, show you have understood by writing '**vor**' '**hinter**' or '**neben**' in the correct box. You may put **V**, **H**, or **N** for short.

Beispiel:
Die Kirche ist vor der Burg.

You write **V** in the box along from 'Kirche' and down from 'Burg'.

	Bahnhof	Burg	Kino	Museum	Rathaus	Schwimmbad
Kirche		V				
Park						
Marktplatz						
Post						
Toilette						
Sportplatz						

Und jetzt du!

Follow the instructions in number order.

A is looking for the church.

1 Say 'Entschuldigung' (*excuse me*).
3 Ask where the church is.
5 Say thank you and goodbye.

B is a passer-by.

2 Say yes?
4 Find the answer on your grid, and tell **A**.
6 Say not at all.

Now make up similar dialogues using the information on the grid. There are twelve possible dialogues.

22   Wie weit ist das?   22

Germans and other Europeans measure distances in metres (**Meter**) and kilometres (**Kilometer**). They do not use miles or yards, feet, and inches. So to understand distances, you need to have some idea what these measurements mean. You have probably learnt about them already, but if you have forgotten, perhaps these diagrams will help.

```
_____   ein Kilometer
_____   eine Meile
```

8 Kilometer sind 5 Meilen.
1 Kilometer ist ⅝ Meile.

```
_____   ein Yard
_____   ein Meter
```

1 Kilometer hat 1000 Meter.
½ Kilometer hat 500 Meter.

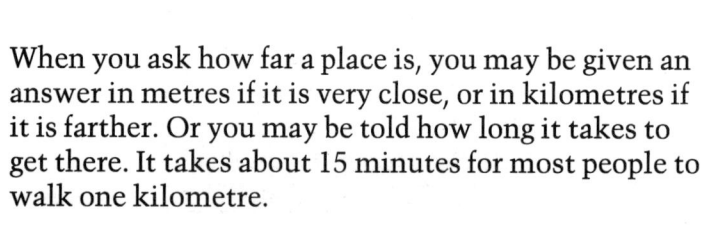

When you ask how far a place is, you may be given an answer in metres if it is very close, or in kilometres if it is farther. Or you may be told how long it takes to get there. It takes about 15 minutes for most people to walk one kilometre.

Write down these figures. Your teacher will then read them out in a different order. Tick them as you hear them.

50	100	150	200	250
300	350	400	450	500
550	600	650	700	750
800	850	900	950	1000

✏ Und jetzt du!

Imagine you are travelling in Germany. You see these signs. Work out how far each town is in miles, and tell your friend in German.

Beispiel: Homburg ist 8 Kilometer.
               Das sind 5 Meilen.

66

	Was?	Wie?	
	ask if it is far	Ist das weit?	
say it's only 5 minutes	on foot	Nein, nur fünf Minuten	zu Fuß.
	by bus		mit dem Bus.
	say it's quite a way	Ja, ziemlich weit.	
say it's about	1 kilometre	Ungefähr ein Kilometer.	
	100 metres	Hundert Meter.	
	500 metres	Fünfhundert Meter.	

Kapiert?

How far is each place?

Choose your answer from the box. You need only write the correct letter next to the number of the question.

1 das Rathaus
2 die Toilette
3 die Post
4 der Bahnhof
5 die Burg
6 das Kino
7 die Disco
8 das Museum
9 die Kirche
10 der Park

A	100 Meter
B	200 Meter
C	500 Meter
D	1 Kilometer
E	2 Kilometer
F	5 Kilometer
G	5 Minuten zu Fuß
H	10 Minuten zu Fuß
I	5 Minuten mit dem Bus
J	10 Minuten mit dem Bus

Und jetzt du!

Imagine you and your partner are standing in front of this big plan of a town you are visiting.

A: Ask where the castle is.
B: Point to it and say 'here'.
A: Ask if it is far.
B: Read the distance off the circle.

Take turns to be **A** and **B** and make up lots of similar conversations.

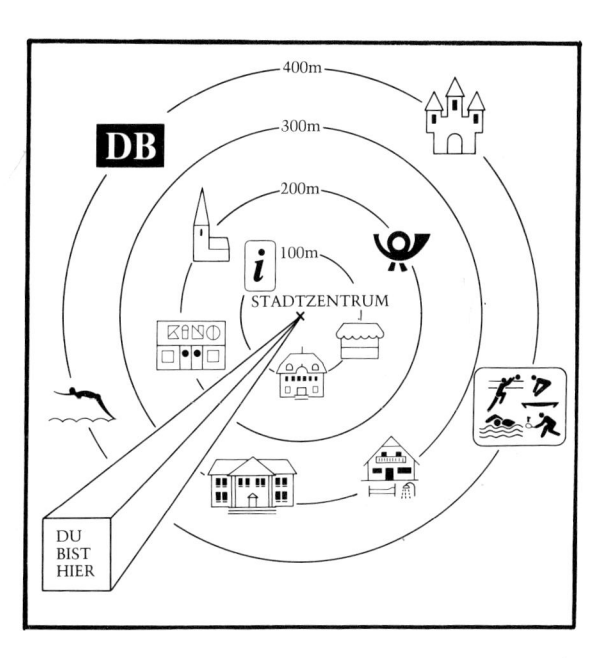

Stadtplan Cochem

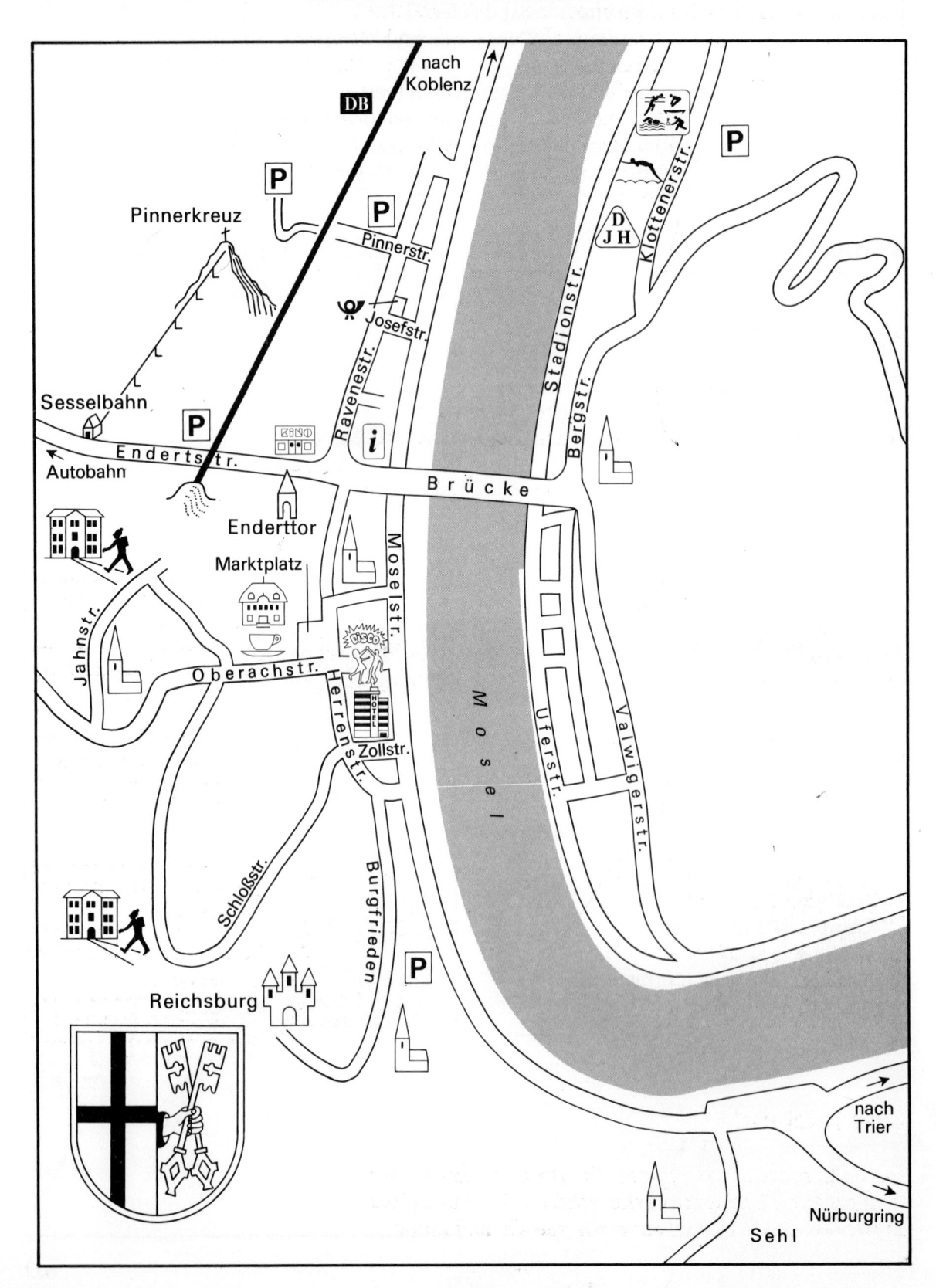

Was?	Wie?
say you would like (to do) something	Ich möchte ...
to see a film	einen Film sehen
to drink a beer	ein Bier trinken
information	Information
to take a train	mit dem Zug fahren
to eat something	etwas essen
to play football	Fußball spielen
to buy stamps	Briefmarken kaufen
to dance	tanzen
to swim	schwimmen

Ich möchte ...

These children all want to do different things.
Try to work out what exactly each wants to do, then look at the map opposite to see where he or she should go.
You will need to use your intelligence to guess some of the new words. If you are stuck, look them up at the back of the book.

> Ich möchte schwimmen gehen.

Du: In der Klottenerstraße ist ein Schwimmbad.

> Wo ist das genau?

Du: Vor dem Sportplatz.

> Ich möchte einen Film sehen.

Du: In der Endertstraße ist ein __.

> Wo ist das genau?

Du: Gegenüber dem __.

> Ich möchte tanzen.

Du: In der Herrenstraße ist eine __.

> Wo ist das genau?

Du: Neben dem __.

> Ich möchte ein Bier trinken.

Du: Auf dem Marktplatz ist ein __.

> Wo ist das genau?

Neben dem __.

Und jetzt du!

Make up more conversations like the ones above with your partner. Use some of the words and phrases given in the box above as well as words you already know.

24 Du, Sie und ihr 24

i As you know, **du** means 'you'. However, you only use it if you are talking to one person, usually a friend or relation whom you call by his or her first name. You also use it if you are talking to a pet.

Beispiele: Mutti
Vati
Onkel Heinrich
Susi
Martin
Rosa (der Hamster)

If you are talking to several of these together, or writing them a letter, you address them as **ihr**.

If however you are talking or writing to a total stranger, or to someone you would not call by his or her first name, then the word for 'you' is **Sie**. It is *always* written with a capital letter. It can be used when talking to one person or to several.

Du bist mein bester Freund.

*Cochem, den 9. August
Liebe Mama, lieber Papa,
Ihr werdet sicher staunen, einen Brief von mir zu bekommen.*

Und jetzt du!

How would you address these people if you were German?

1 your friend
2 your brothers
3 your teacher
4 a policeman
5 an uncle
6 your cat
7 your mum
8 the grocer
9 your class
10 a passer-by

Sagen Sie bitte, wo ist der Bahnhof?

ACHTUNG!

If you meet a boy or girl your own age, or younger, you say **du** even before you know their first name.

ACHTUNG!

du	Sie
Woher komm**st** du?	Woher komm**en** Sie?
Wo wohn**st** du?	Wo wohn**en** Sie?
Was möch**test** du?	Was möch**ten** Sie?
Wohin will**st** du?	Wohin woll**en** Sie?

70

25 — Wie komme ich am besten zu ...? — 25

Sie gehen links.
Du gehst links.

Sie gehen rechts.
Du gehst rechts.

Sie gehen geradeaus.
Du gehst geradeaus.

Sie gehen hier entlang
| bis zum ____.
| bis zur ____.

Du gehst hier entlang
| bis zum ____.
| bis zur ____.

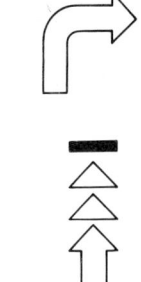

ACHTUNG!
Look carefully to see whether to use **zum** or **zur** to mean 'to the'.
If you want to know how to decide for yourself which to use, see page 144.

Das ist neu

die Ampel
bis zur Ampel

die Kreuzung
bis zur Kreuzung

die Ecke
bis zur Ecke

& und dann

WI-Bierstadt   WI-Erbenheim
Kurhaus   Hauptbhf.

Zum Ausfüllen

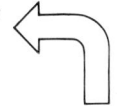

1. Entschuldigung. Wie komme ich am besten zur P___?
   Du gehst l____.

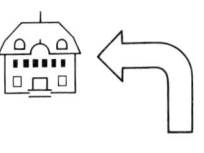

2. Entschuldigung. Wie komme ___ __ besten zum R_____?
   & Sie gehen g_____ und dann l____.

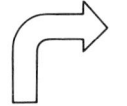

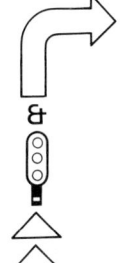

3. Entschuldigung. Wie _____ ich am _____ zum B_____?
   Du _____ rechts.

4. _____. ___ komme ich am besten zur B___?
   Sie _____ hier entlang b__ zur Ampel und dann rechts.

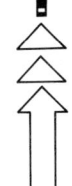

71

🎧 Und jetzt du!

> **Du** with first names
> **Sie** with surnames
>
> Hans   Susi
> Herr Braun   Heidi
> Fräulein Böll Frau Mayer
> Lothar

Partner **A:** choose a name from the box.
Partner **B:** ask where **A** wants to go. Be sure to use the right word for 'you'.

Beispiel:
Wohin **willst du**, Hans?
Wohin **wollen Sie**, Herr Braun?

Partner **A:** choose a place from the boxes below and say it, together with the right word for 'to the' (**zum** or **zur**).

Partner **B:** tell **A** which way to go. Refer to the symbols below. Use the correct word for 'you':

Beispiel:
Du gehst links.
Sie gehen links.

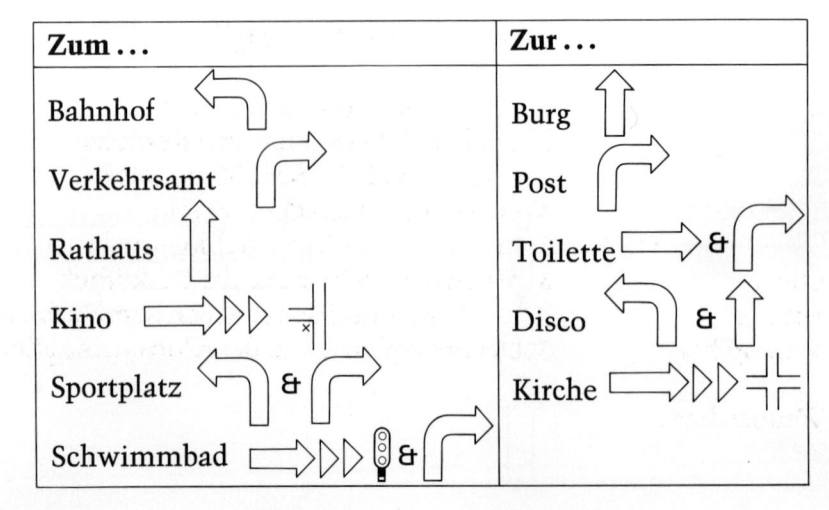

⊛ Kapiert?

Wohin willst du?
Listen to these nine people asking the way. Draw your own grid. First fill in where the person is going under '**wohin**?' then tick the right column to show which way they should go. You may need more than one tick for complicated directions.

wohin?	⬅	⬆	➡
1			
2			
3			
4			
5			
6			
7			
8			
9			

Zum ...	Zur ...
Bahnhof	Burg
Verkehrsamt	Post
Rathaus	Toilette
Kino	Disco
Sportplatz	Kirche
Schwimmbad	

Wiederholung Fünf

Kapiert?

As you listen, make rough notes about where each person wants to go, where that is and how best to get there. Use a chart like this to record your answers.

	Herr Werner	Paula	Manuel	Frau Bolzer
Going to?				
Where is it?				
What directions?				

> Cochem, den 4. Mai
>
> Liebe Ute,
>
> Danke für Deinen Brief. Ich wohne in Cochem. Das ist in Westdeutschland, an der Mosel. Cochem ist nicht weit von Koblenz, nur sechzig Kilometer. Hier ist ein Stadtplan. Ich wohne in der Ravenestraße, zwischen der Post und der Polizeiwache. Das ist nicht weit vom Busbahnhof und dem Verkehrsamt. Meine Schule ist in der Schloßstraße. Das sind nur zehn Minuten zu Fuß. Samstags gehe ich oft in eine Diskothek. Die Disco ist in der Herrenstraße. Der Eintritt kostet 4 DM. Mittwochs gehe ich immer ins Schwimmbad. Das ist neben dem Sportplatz in der Klottenerstraße.
>
> Und wie ist's bei Dir?
>
> Viele Grüße
> Deine Martina

True or false?

1. Ute is writing to Martina.
2. It is May 4th.
3. Martina lives in Cochem.
4. Cochem is twenty kilometres away from Koblenz.
5. She lives near the post office.
6. Her school is in Englandstraße.
7. It takes five minutes to walk to her school.
8. She goes swimming on Wednesdays.

Falsch oder richtig?

1. Martina kommt aus Cochem.
2. Cochem ist sehr weit von Koblenz.
3. Martina wohnt in der Moselstraße.
4. Sie wohnt neben der Post.
5. Ihre Schule ist in der Schloßstraße.
6. Mittwochs geht sie in die Diskothek.
7. Das Schwimmbad ist neben dem Rathaus.
8. Der Sportplatz ist in der Klottenerstraße.

NOW YOU ARE READY FOR WAYSTAGE 5.

26 — Wie fährt man in Deutschland? — 26

Man kann mit dem Bus fahren.
Hier ist eine Bushaltestelle.

Das ist ein Klappbus. Das ist in Bochum.

Eine Busfahrkarte ist billig.
Hier ist ein Automat.

Dort drüben ist der Busbahnhof.
Das ist in Betzdorf.

Man kann mit der Straßenbahn fahren.
Hier ist ein Straßenbahn aus Bochum.

So steigt man ein.

Hier ist der Hauptbahnhof in Hamburg. Herr Kröger fährt mit dem Zug.

In Hamburg sind eine S-Bahn (Stadtbahn) und eine U-Bahn (Untergrundbahn).

Oft fahren Deutsche mit dem Schiff. Das ist in Cochem, an der Mosel.

Aber natürlich kann man auch mit dem Auto fahren oder radfahren.

Oder sogar zu Fuß gehen

wie hier in Trier.

27   Stadtplan Wiesbaden   27

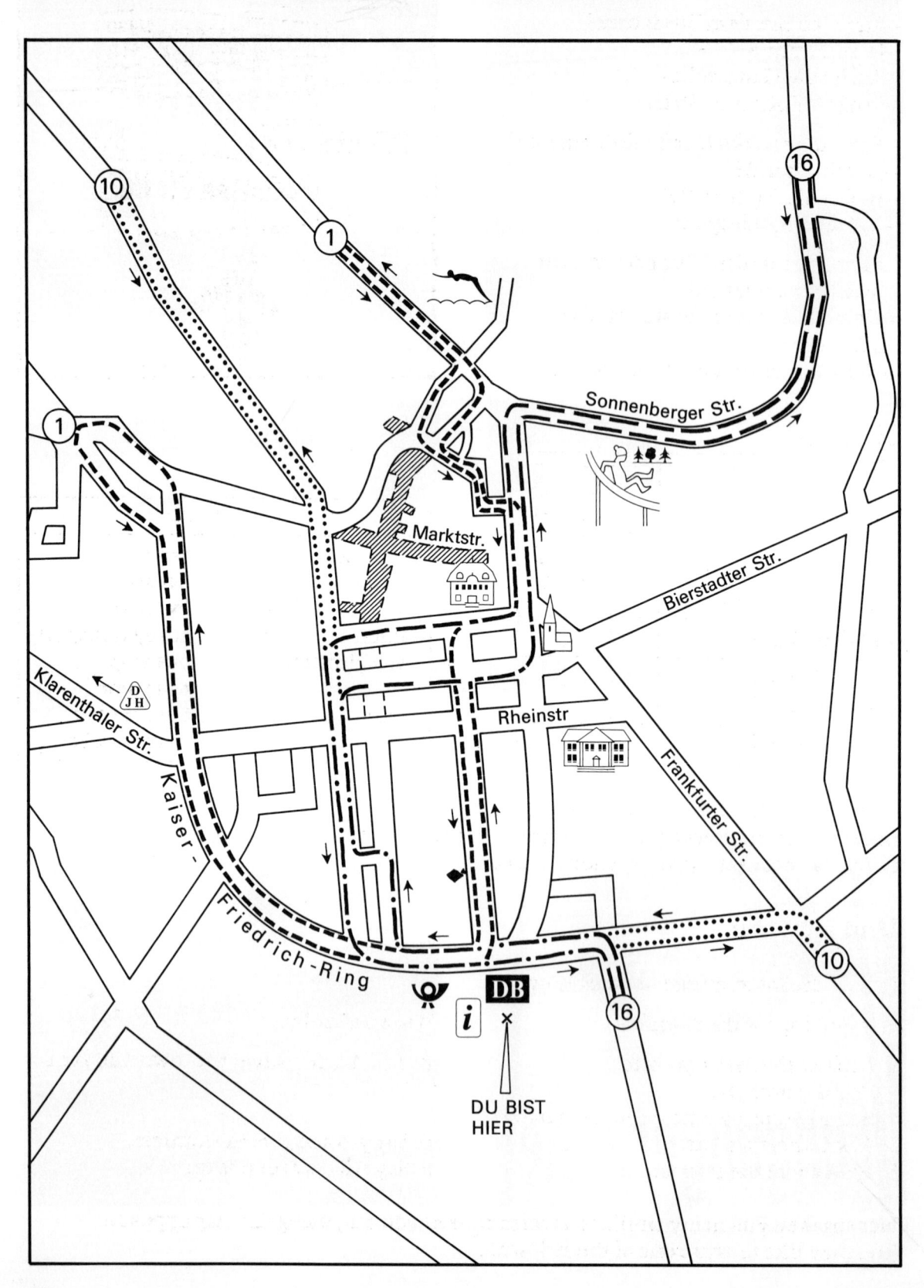

DU BIST HIER

Wie komme ich dahin?

–Kann ich mit dem Bus fahren?
–Ja, mit Linie 8.
–Wo ist die Haltestelle?
–In der Münchener Straße.

–Kann ich mit der Straßenbahn fahren?
–Ja, mit Linie 23.
–Wo ist die Haltestelle?
–Auf dem Bundesplatz.

–Kann ich mit dem Bus oder mit der Straßenbahn fahren?
–Nein, du gehst am besten zu Fuß.
 oder
–Nein, Sie gehen am besten zu Fuß.

Kapiert?

	Bahnhof	Burg	Rathaus	Stadtzentrum	Schwimmbad
mit dem Bus					
mit der Straßenbahn					
zu Fuß					

Das ist neu	
kann ich?	can I?
mit dem Bus	by bus
mit der Straßenbahn	by tram
fahren	go (by transport)
die Haltestelle	bus stop
	tram stop
Linie	bus number
	tram number

Copy this grid. As you listen, show you have understood where each person wants to go and how he or she can best get there by ticking the appropriate box.

Und jetzt du!

Follow the instructions in number order.

A is looking for the town hall.

B is a passer-by.

1 Look at the map opposite.
  You are here: ×.
  Ask a passer-by where the town hall is.

2 Tell **A** what street the town hall is in.

3 Ask if there's a bus.

4 Say yes and give the number.

5 Ask where the stop is.

6 Say what street it is in.

Now make up as many similar conversations as you can, using the map opposite.
You may like to write one of them down.

Konversation

Herr Mayer: Entschuldigung. Ich will zum Rathaus. Wie komme ich am besten dahin?
Frau Krall: Zum Rathaus? Das ist in der Konrad Adenauer Straße.
Herr Mayer: Ist das weit?
Frau Krall: Ja, ziemlich. Ungefähr einen Kilometer.
Herr Mayer: Kann ich mit dem Bus fahren?
Frau Krall: Ja, mit Linie 11.
Herr Mayer: Und wo ist die Haltestelle?
Frau Krall: Am Dresdener Platz.
Herr Mayer: Wo ist das genau?
Frau Krall: Sie gehen hier entlang bis zur Ampel, dann rechts. Der Dresdener Platz ist gleich da.
Herr Mayer: So. Recht schönen Dank.
Frau Krall: Bitte sehr.
Herr Mayer: Auf Wiedersehen.
Frau Krall: Auf Wiedersehen.

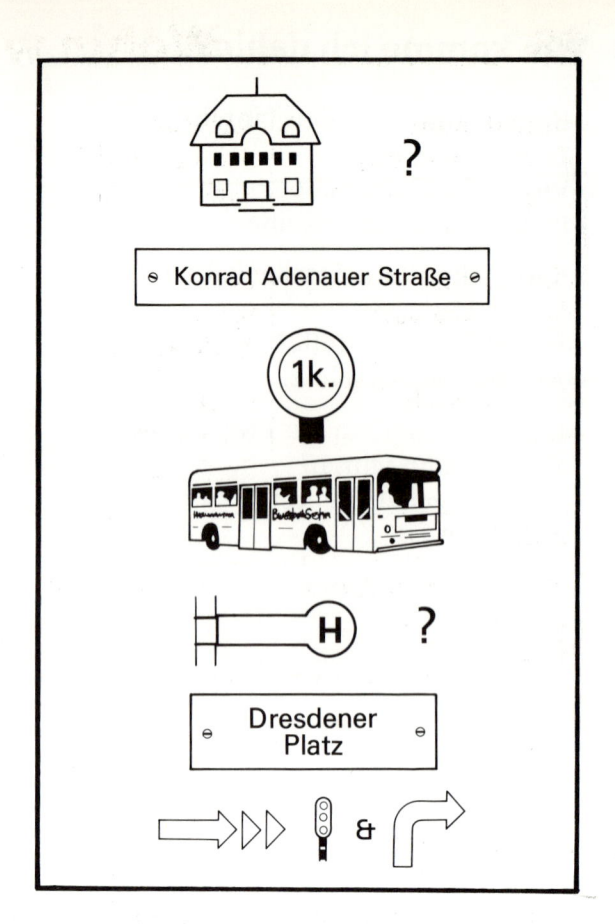

Kapiert?

Listen to the conversation printed above. Copy the statements printed below. After each one write **Richtig** or **Falsch**. If you can, you can then write correct statements to replace the ones that were wrong.

1 Herr Mayer will zum Museum.
2 Das Museum ist in der Konrad Adenauer Straße.
3 Das ist weit – ungefähr zwei Kilometer.
4 Er kann mit dem Bus fahren.
5 Buslinie 12 fährt zum Rathaus.
6 Die Haltestelle ist in der Dresdener Straße.
7 Herr Mayer muß bis zur Kreuzung gehen, und dann rechts.
8 Frau Krall sagt bitte.

ACHTUNG!

du gehst   du fährst

Sie gehen   Sie fahren

28 Wohin willst du? 28

Ich will **zum** | Rathaus
(zu dem) | Schwimmbad
                   | Park

Ich will **zur** | Post
(zu der) | Schule
                   | Toilette

Ich will **nach** | Bonn
                   | Nierstein
                   | England

ACHTUNG!

Two of the ways of saying 'to' in German are '**nach**' and '**zu**'.

Use **nach** with names of countries, towns and villages.
Otherwise use **zu**.

Und jetzt du!

Tell your partner you want to go to these places.
He or she will tell you how best to get there.

Beispiel:

A: Ich will zum Museum.
B: Du fährst am besten mit dem Bus.

1 zur

2 zum

3 zum

4 zur

5 zum

6 zur

29 Ist das der Bus ...?

— Ist das der Bus zum Hauptbahnhof?
— Ja.

— Ist das der Zug nach Oldenburg?
— Nein, der fährt nach Bremerhaven.

— Ist das das Schiff nach Koblenz?
— Ja, natürlich.

— Ist das die Straßenbahn zum Schwimmbad?
— Nein, Linie 205 fährt zum Schwimmbad.

Kapiert?

Falsch oder richtig?

1 Die Straßenbahn fährt zum Rathaus.
2 Der Bus fährt zum Sportplatz.
3 Der Zug fährt nach Münster.
4 Die Straßenbahn fährt zum Stadtzentrum.
5 Der Zug fährt nach Essen.
6 Der Bus fährt zur Burg.
7 Die Straßenbahn fährt zum Rathaus.
8 Der Bus fährt nach Freiburg.

Und jetzt du!

Decide where you want to go from the places at the ends of the lines. Then in turns, ask each other if the bus or tram you are pointing to is the right one for where you want to go. If it is not, your partner should tell you the right one to catch.

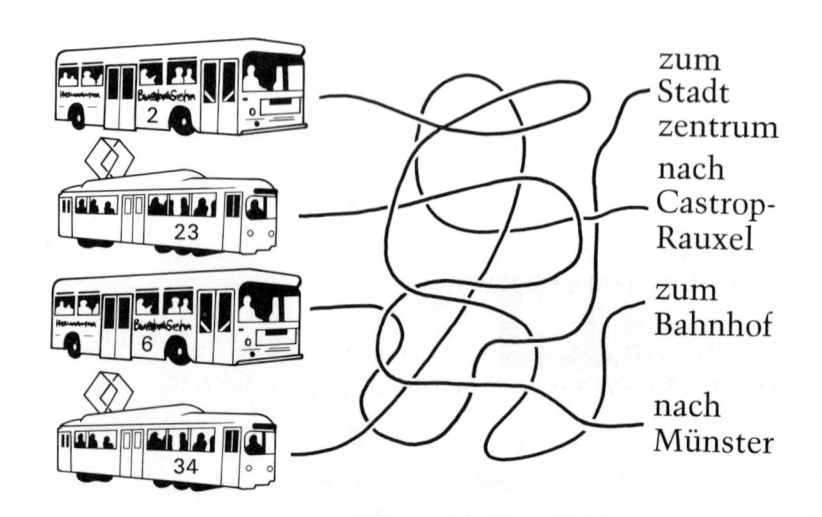

zum Stadtzentrum

nach Castrop-Rauxel

zum Bahnhof

nach Münster

Beispiel:

— Ist das die Straßenbahn nach Castrop–Rauxel?

— Nein, die fährt zum Bahnhof. Linie 34 fährt nach Castrop–Rauxel.

Kapiert?

These people are at the **Verkehrsamt** (tourist information). They are enquiring about transport to various places. Tick the chart to show you understand what means of transport they are using and fill in the bus or tram number under 'Linie'.

	Wohin?	Bus	Straßenbahn	Linie
1				
2				
3				
4				
5				

Was?	**Wie?**
ask which bus goes there	Welcher Bus fährt dahin?
ask which tram goes there	Welche Straßenbahn fährt dahin?
ask which number bus or tram	Welche Linie?
ask how to get to a place	Wie komme ich zum ____?
	Wie komme ich zur ____?
	Wie komme ich nach ____?
tell someone to go by bus	Sie fahren am besten mit dem Bus.
	Du fährst am besten mit dem Bus.

Und jetzt du!

Follow the instructions in number order.

A is a tourist.

1 Say hello, excuse me.
3 Ask how to get to the swimming pool.
5 Ask which tram.
7 Say thank you, goodbye.

B works in Verkehrsamt Bochum.

2 Say hello.
4 Tell **A** to go by tram.
6 Tell **A** it's the number 6.
8 Say not at all, goodbye.

Now make up similar conversations asking about transport to other places on the chart you filled in above.

30   Wann fährt der Zug?   30

It is not enough to know which bus or train to get if you don't know when it leaves. This is how you ask in German.

3:00

Wann fährt der Bus?
Wann fährt der Bus Linie 12?
– Um drei Uhr.

7:30

Wann fährt der Zug?
Wann fährt der Zug nach Dresden?
– Um sieben Uhr dreißig.

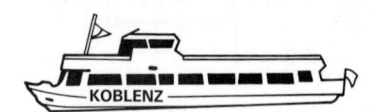

10:20

Wann fährt das Schiff?
Wann fährt das Schiff nach Koblenz?
– Um zehn Uhr zwanzig.

8:25

Wann fährt die Straßenbahn?
Wann fährt die Straßenbahn Linie 34?
– Um acht Uhr fünfundzwanzig.

Und jetzt du!

Ask each other when these are leaving.
Give the right answer, as in the example.

Beispiel:

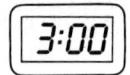

3:00   Wann fährt der Bus Linie 13?
– Um drei Uhr.

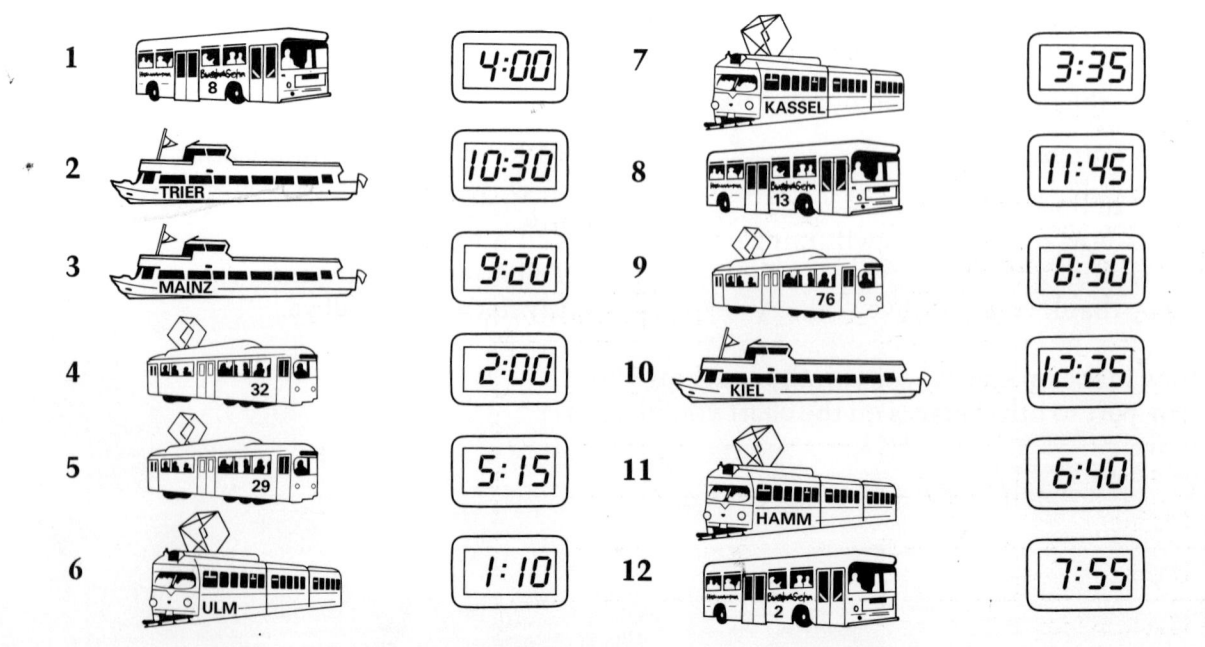

1. 4:00
2. 10:30
3. 9:20
4. 2:00
5. 5:15
6. 1:10
7. 3:35
8. 11:45
9. 8:50
10. 12:25
11. 6:40
12. 7:55

Und wann kommt er an?

Here is how you ask for the time of arrival:

⟹ Katzwinkel   ⟹ Bonn

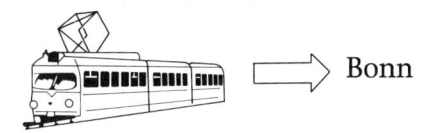

Wann `kommt` der Bus in Katzwinkel `an`? Wann `kommt` der Zug in Bonn `an`?

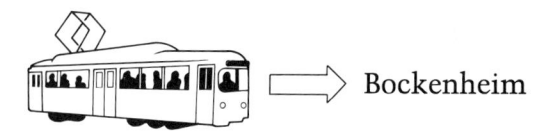

⟹ Trier   ⟹ Bockenheim

Wann `kommt` das Schiff in Trier `an`? Wann `kommt` die Straßenbahn in Bockenheim `an`?

And this is what the answer might be:

Um drei Uhr zwanzig. `3:20`

Um fünf Uhr zehn. `5:10`

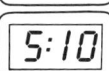

Um elf Uhr dreiundvierzig. `11:43`

Gleis 6 — Abfahrt 13:56 — Mainz — Hält nicht überall — Nahverkehrszug

Kapiert?

Are these trains about to arrive or to leave?
Write the numbers 1–10 and after each number
put **A** for arriving or **L** for leaving.

Und noch mehr!

When will these people leave, and when will they reach their destinations? Copy the chart. Under 'Transportmittel' fill in the means of transport.

Nach	Abfahrt	Ankunft	Transportmittel
Köln	7.30	8.14	Zug
Berlin			
Bonn			
Mainz			
Bremen			
Gartenstadt			

83

9 Und jetzt du!

Take turns to ask each other when the following reach their destinations, and to give the correct reply.

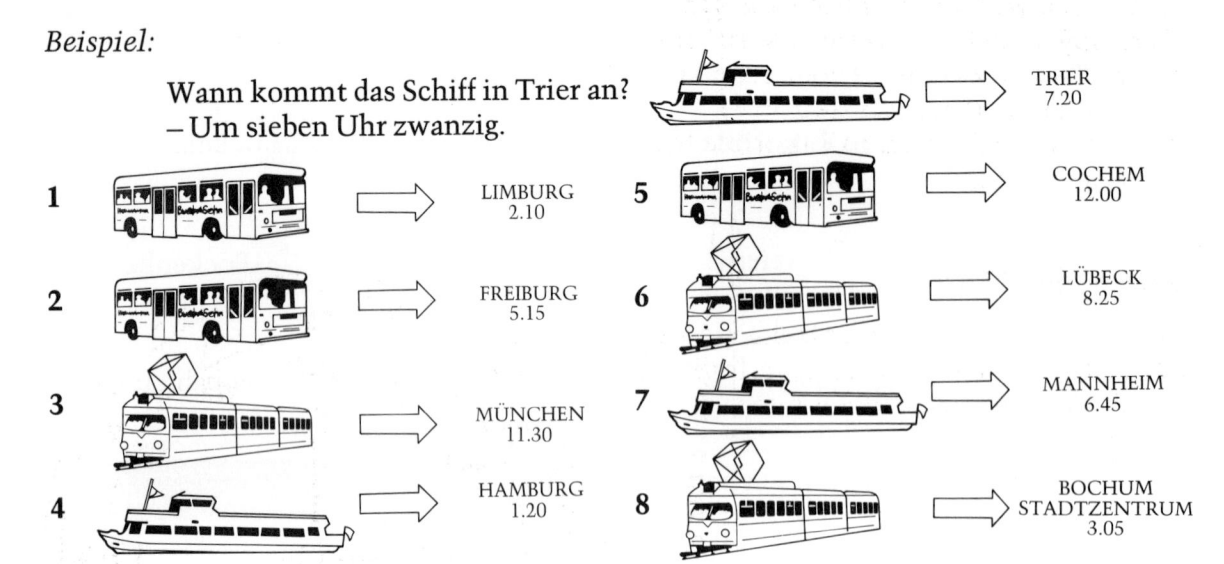

Beispiel:

Wann kommt das Schiff in Trier an?
– Um sieben Uhr zwanzig.

1 → LIMBURG 2.10
2 → FREIBURG 5.15
3 → MÜNCHEN 11.30
4 → HAMBURG 1.20
5 → COCHEM 12.00
6 → LÜBECK 8.25
7 → MANNHEIM 6.45
8 → BOCHUM STADTZENTRUM 3.05

Wann fährt das Schiff?

20:15 die bekannte Große ABENDFAHRT bei Wein, Musik und Tanz nach BEILSTEIN mit Schleusenfahrt und zurück 22:30 Fahrpreis DM 9,- Kinder halber Fahrpreis Achtung im Vorverkauf bis 18:00 nur DM 8,- Preiswerte Restauration an Bord Personenschiffahrt KOLB 5591 Briedern - Tel.: 02673/347

This is a board advertising a boat trip.

Antworte auf englisch:

1 At what time of day is the trip?
2 What can you do during the trip?
3 At what time does it leave?
4 When does it return?
5 What does the trip cost?
6 Are there any reductions?

31 ──────── Wie spät ist es? ──────── 31

Did you notice that the advertisement on page 84 shows times using the 24-hour clock? You will find that timetables in Germany, as in Britain, often use it. This means that times after 12 noon are given as 13.00 to 24.00 hours instead of as 1 p.m. to 12 p.m. Germans do not use the terms a.m. or p.m.

Wie spät ist es?

1 7.15 = sieben Uhr fünfzehn morgens
2 13.20 = ein Uhr zwanzig nachmittags
3 21.30 = neun Uhr dreißig abends
4 22.15 =
5 23.00 =
6 14.20 =
7 8.35 =
8 18.40 =
9 17.10 =
10 4.04 =
11 2.57 =
12 16.32 =
13 15.45 =
14 19.05 =
15 11.15 =

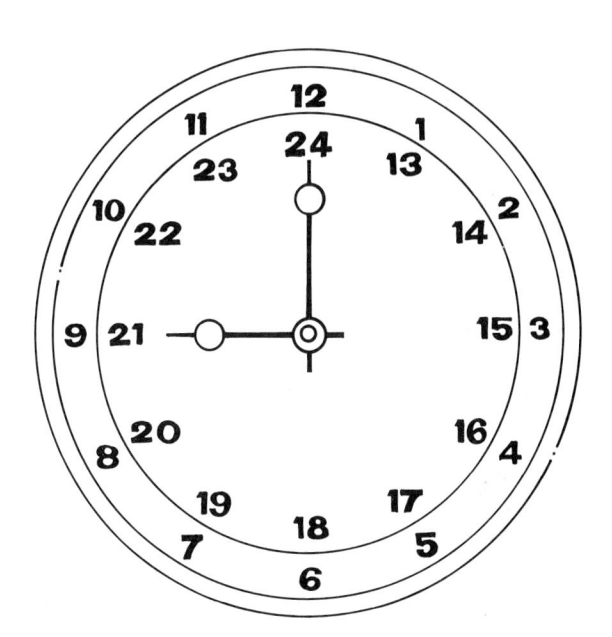

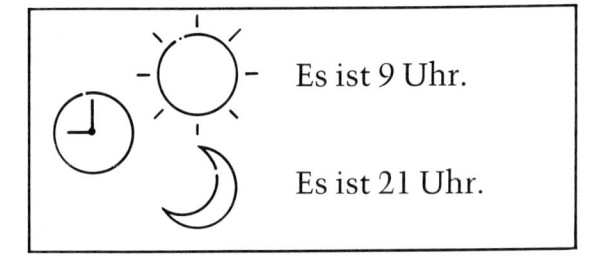

Es ist 9 Uhr.

Es ist 21 Uhr.

Kapiert?

Do these trains leave before or after midday?

	1	2	3	4	5	6	7	8	9	10
Before midday										
After midday										

Fahrplan

km	Koblenz 226 ab	Zug	Karlsruhe an	Bemerkungen
	0.53	D	201 3.26	
①	6.09	E	2257 9.26	🍷
	6.40	IC	565 8.58	Ⓤ Mainz Ⓤ Mannh
②	6.51	IC	511 8.58	Ⓤ Mannh
	7.51		105 9.58	
	8.51	IC	117 10.58	Ⓤ Mannh
②	9.51	IC	513 11.58	Ⓤ Mannh
	10.27	FD	703 12.47	✕
	10.34	D	701 12.53	🍷
	10.51	IC	107 12.58	
	11.41		7 13.47	
	11.51	IC	515 13.58	Ⓤ Mannh
	12.03	D	407 14.27	✕
	12.51	IC	517 14.58	Ⓤ Mannh
	13.10	D	203 15.23	✕
	13.51	IC	613 15.58	Ⓤ Mannh
	14.09	D	705 16.29	🍷
	14.51	IC	611 16.58	Ⓤ Mannh
	15.24	D	725 18.36	🍽🍷
③	15.51	IC	519 17.58	Ⓤ Mannh
	15.51	IC	519 18.36	Ⓤ Mainz
	16.24	D	207 19.24	🍷
	16.51	IC	615 18.58	Ⓤ Mannh
	17.51	IC	109 19.58	
	18.51	IC	617 20.58	Ⓤ Mannh
	19.48	D	205 22.29	🍷
③	19.51	IC	619 21.58	Ⓤ Mannh
	20.51	IC	132 22.58	81

① = ① bis ⑥
② = ① bis ⑥, auch 00.00., nicht 18. VI.
③ = täglich ausser ⑥, auch 00.00., nicht 17. VI.
81 = ⑥, ⑦ Karlsruhe an 23.03

What do you think these symbols mean? Match up the symbol with its meaning.

1 TEE   a restaurant car
2 Ⓤ Mannh   b drinks available
3 E   c intercity train
4 🍷   d change at Mannheim
5 an   e D-ZUG (express)
6 D   f Eilzug
7 km 226   g Transeuropean Express
8 ab   h 226 kilometres
9 ✕   i departs
10 IC   j arrives

Study the timetable above. Can you choose the most appropriate train?

1 You want to go to Karlsruhe, leaving around 8 a.m.
   a What time does the train leave?
   b Do you have to change at Mannheim?
   c Is it an intercity train?
   d When will you reach Karlsruhe?

2 You want to go to Karlsruhe, leaving around midday. You want to eat on the train, so it must have a dining car.
   a What time does your train leave?
   b Do you have to change?
   c When will you arrive?

3 You want to go to Karlsruhe, leaving between 4 p.m. and 5 p.m. You don't want to have to change trains.
   a What time can you leave?
   b Is it an intercity train?
   c Can you get refreshments on the train?
   d When will you arrive?

4 You want to go to Karlsruhe, leaving as late as possible.
   a What time must you leave?
   b When will you arrive?
   c What type of train is it?
   d Can you get food or drink on it?

Kapiert?

Write down the times of departure and arrival.

Nach	Abfahrt	Ankunft
Bonn		
Hamburg		
Koblenz		
Köln		
Bremen		
Siegen		

Was?	Wie?
say you want to go somewhere	Ich will nach Karlsruhe.
ask how to get there	Wie komme ich dahin?
ask when the train leaves	Wann fährt der Zug?
ask when it gets there	Wann kommt der Zug in ____ an?

Und jetzt du!

Using the timetable opposite, work out this conversation in pairs. Imagine it is 10 a.m.

Follow the instructions in number order.

A is a passenger.
1 Say you want to go to Karlsruhe.
3 Ask when the train leaves.
5 Ask when it arrives.
7 Say thank you.

B is a railway clerk.
2 Say yes?
4 Say at 10.27.
6 Say at 12.47.
8 Say not at all.

Now make up similar conversations at these times:

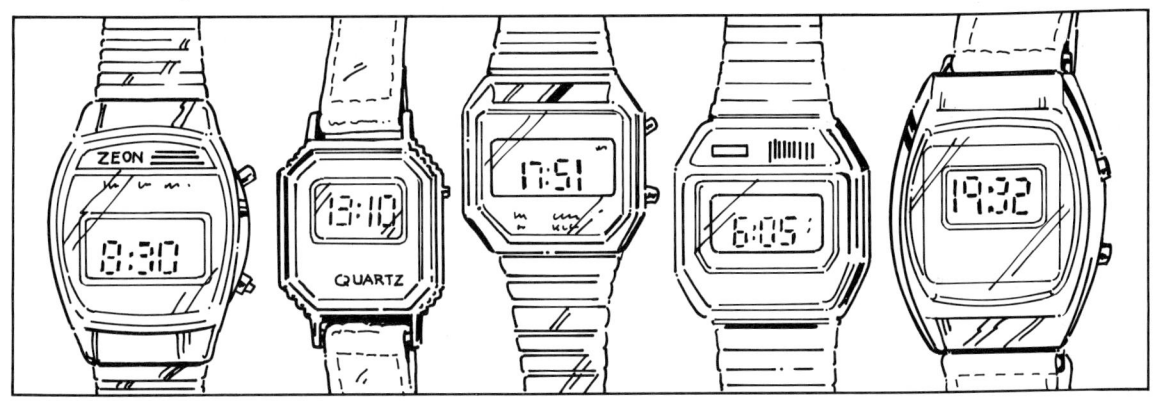

8:30   13:10   17:51   6:05   19:32

32 — Einmal nach Hannover, bitte — 32

Einmal nach Hannover, einfach. → HANNOVER

Einmal nach Hannover, hin und zurück. ↔ HANNOVER

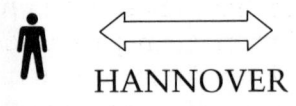

Zweimal nach Hannover, einfach. → HANNOVER

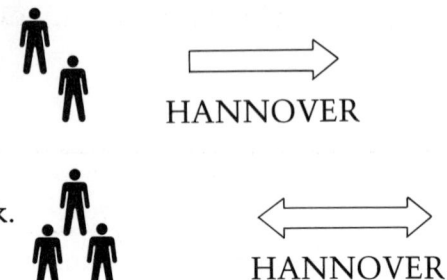

Dreimal nach Hannover, hin und zurück. ↔ HANNOVER

Kapiert?

How many tickets does each person buy? Number your answers 1–8.
Are they single or return tickets? Listen again, and put **S** or **R** after each answer.

Und jetzt du!

In turn, ask your partner for these tickets.
Your partner should make up a price.

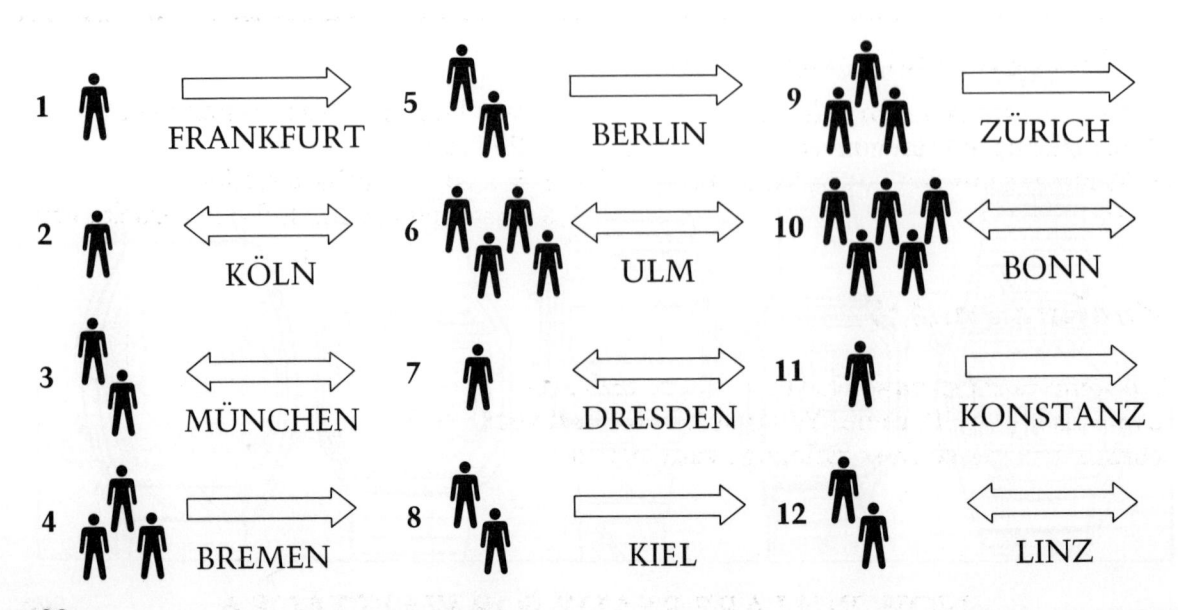

1. → FRANKFURT
2. ↔ KÖLN
3. ↔ MÜNCHEN
4. → BREMEN
5. → BERLIN
6. ↔ ULM
7. ↔ DRESDEN
8. → KIEL
9. → ZÜRICH
10. ↔ BONN
11. → KONSTANZ
12. ↔ LINZ

Wiederholung Sechs

Kapiert?

What does each person want to know?
Match the names with the questions.

1 Herr Kahl   a Is there a bus to the museum?
2 Fräulein Schwert   b Which tram goes to the main station?
3 Ludger Saal   c When does the train to Bonn leave?
4 Jutta Kraenke   d Is this the right bus for the town centre?
5 Hannes Liebelt   e How can one get to the castle?
6 Petra Kirschner   f What does a return ticket to Bremen cost?

Bilderrätsel

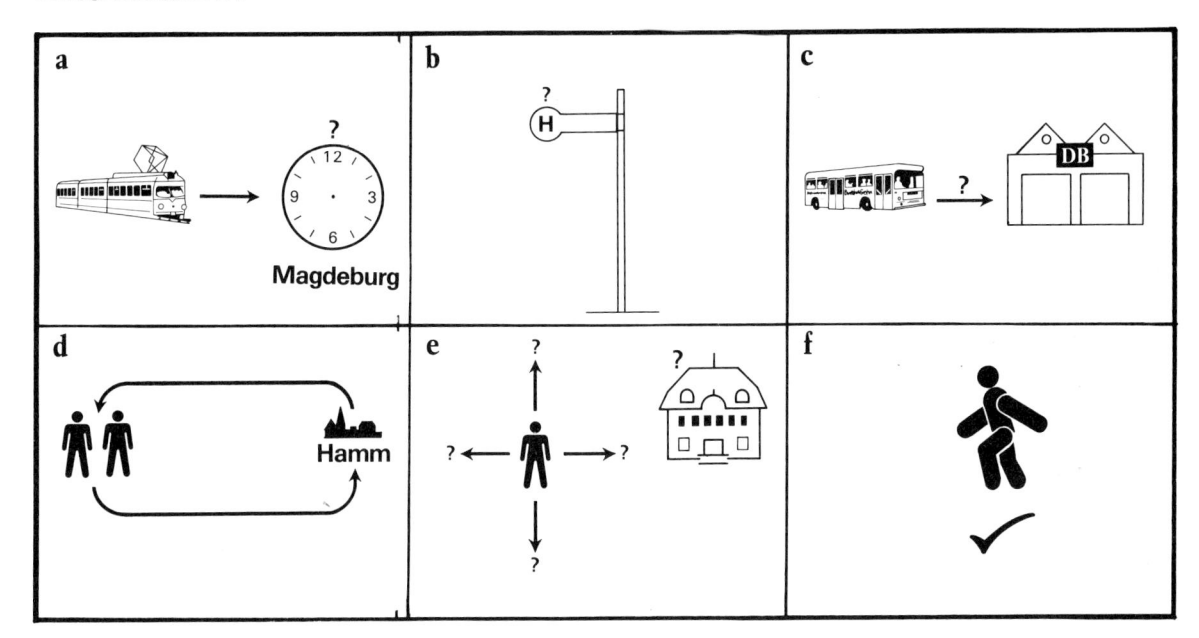

Fit these captions to the right pictures.

1 Fährt dieser Bus zum Bahnhof?
2 Sie gehen am besten zu Fuß.
3 Wann kommt der Zug in Magdeburg an?
4 Wie komme ich am besten zum Rathaus?
5 Wo ist die Bushaltestelle?
6 Zweimal Hamm, hin und zurück, bitte.

Kannst du mehr?

Do some cartoon drawings yourself, and make up captions to go with them. You may like to see if your partner can match the captions to your pictures.

NOW YOU ARE READY FOR WAYSTAGE 6.

33   Geschäfte   33

Hier ist eine deutsche Stadt. Sie heißt Mannheim.
Mannheim ist in Süddeutschland am Rhein.

Das ist die **Bäckerei**.
Hier kauft man Brot und Kuchen, Torte und Brötchen.

Frau Schmidt ist die Bäckerin.

Nebenan ist die **Apotheke**.
In der Apotheke gibt es Medizin und Tabletten.

Frau Klein ist Apothekerin.

Hier ist auch eine **Drogerie**.
Da kauft man Kosmetik, Pflaster, Shampoo und Zahnpasta.

Herr Jung ist der Drogist.

Das hier ist der **Gemüseladen**.
Da gibt es Salat und Tomaten aber auch Äpfel und Bananen.

Der Gemüsehändler heißt Herr Weiß.

Dann gibt es eine **Metzgerei***.
Hier gibt es Fleisch und Wurst.
* Also called **Fleischerei**.

Die Metzgerin heißt Frau Puder.

Das ist die **Post**.
Hier gibt es Briefmarken.
Hier kann man telefonieren und Pakete und Telegramme senden.

Der Postbeamte heißt Herr Förster.

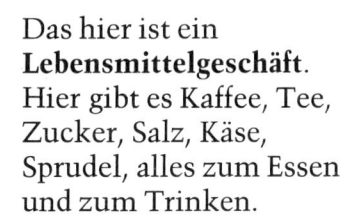

Das hier ist ein **Lebensmittelgeschäft**.
Hier gibt es Kaffee, Tee, Zucker, Salz, Käse, Sprudel, alles zum Essen und zum Trinken.

Lotta Phillip ist die Lebensmittelhändlerin.

Hier ist der **Supermarkt**.
Da kann man viel kaufen.

Der Manager heißt Herr Morgenstern.

Das ist ein **Kaufhaus**.
Das Kaufhaus heißt Kaufhof. Kaufhof gibt es in jeder deutschen Stadt.

Frau Niedermeyer ist die Managerin.

Wo kaufst du das?

List as many shops as possible where you could buy each item.

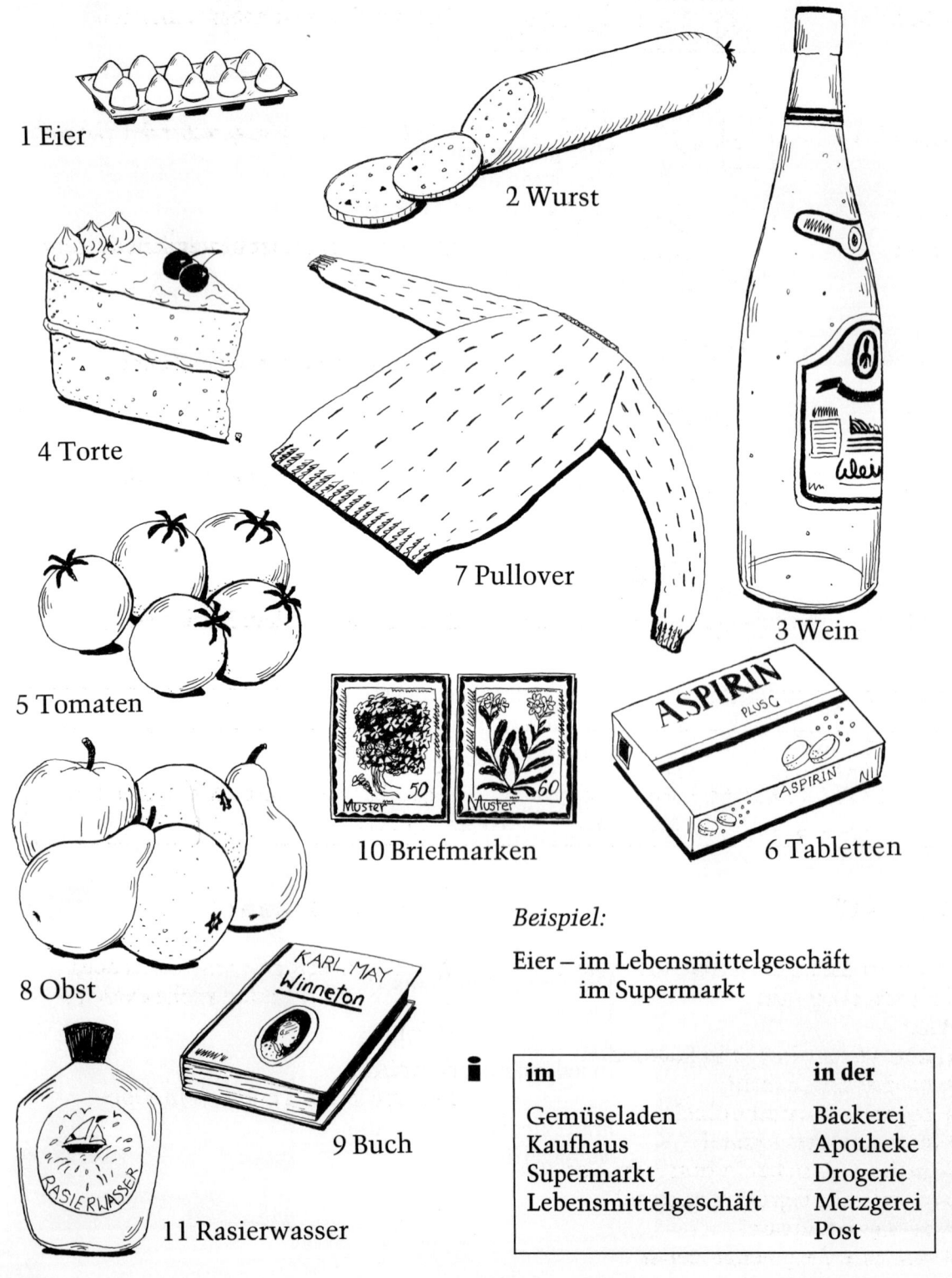

1 Eier

2 Wurst

4 Torte

7 Pullover

3 Wein

5 Tomaten

10 Briefmarken

6 Tabletten

8 Obst

Beispiel:

Eier – im Lebensmittelgeschäft
      im Supermarkt

9 Buch

11 Rasierwasser

im	in der
Gemüseladen	Bäckerei
Kaufhaus	Apotheke
Supermarkt	Drogerie
Lebensmittelgeschäft	Metzgerei
	Post

34 — Wo? — 34

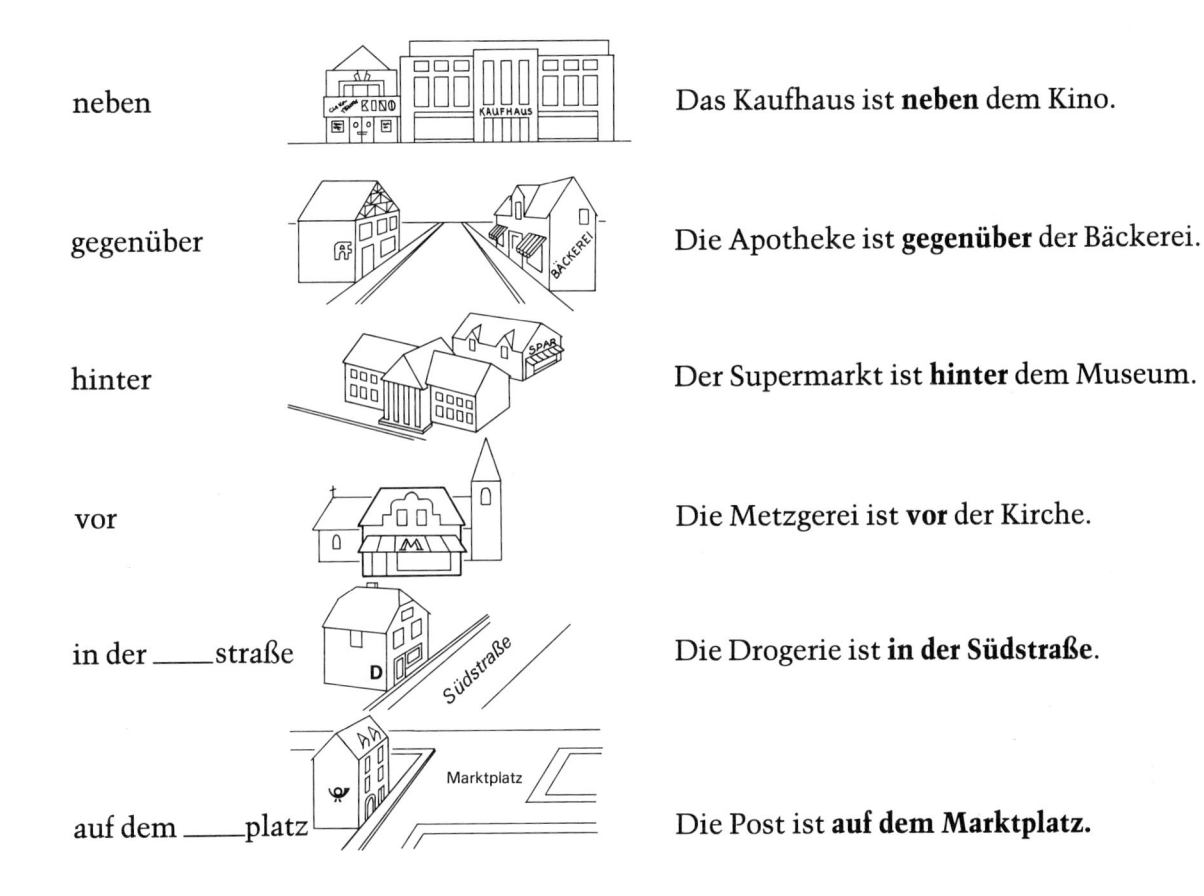

neben — Das Kaufhaus ist **neben** dem Kino.

gegenüber — Die Apotheke ist **gegenüber** der Bäckerei.

hinter — Der Supermarkt ist **hinter** dem Museum.

vor — Die Metzgerei ist **vor** der Kirche.

in der ____straße — Die Drogerie ist **in der Südstraße**.

auf dem ____platz — Die Post ist **auf dem Marktplatz**.

Where's the nearest?			
Wo ist	der die das	nächste	Supermarkt/Gemüseladen? Apotheke/Bäckerei/Drogerie/Fleischerei/Metzgerei/Post? Kaufhaus/Lebensmittelgeschäft?

Kapiert?

Listen to the tape. You are told where different shops are.
What is:
1 next to the cinema in Südstraße?
2 behind the church?
3 opposite the post office?
4 in the market square?
5 in the high street in front of the castle?
6 next to the department store?
7 in Mozart Square?
8 opposite the greengrocer's?

Kannst du mehr?

Write up to eight German sentences using the information in the exercise above.

Beispiel:
Die Drogerie ist neben dem Kino.

Und jetzt du!

Look at the map below. Take it in turns with your partner to find out where the various shops are.
You ask for instance: 'Wo ist der nächste Supermarkt?'
Your partner answers: 'Gegenüber der Bank.'
Your partner scores one point for a correct answer. If he or she fails to answer or makes a mistake, the questioner gets the point.
Keep score like this:

Ich	Mein Partner
I	II

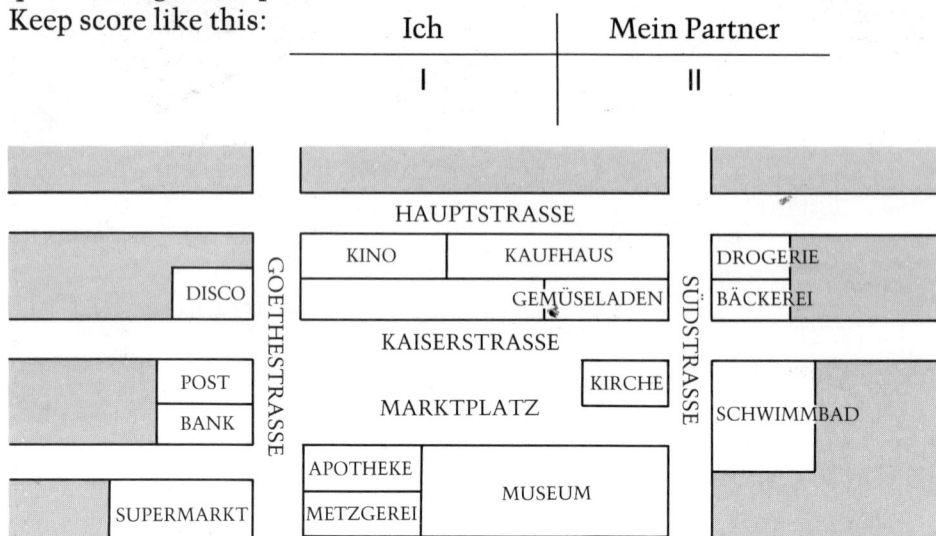

```
                    HAUPTSTRASSE
          KINO  |  KAUFHAUS        DROGERIE
  DISCO                            BÄCKEREI
                   GEMÜSELADEN
                   KAISERSTRASSE
          POST              KIRCHE
                   MARKTPLATZ      SCHWIMMBAD
          BANK
                APOTHEKE
  SUPERMARKT    METZGEREI   MUSEUM
```
(Goethestrasse, Südstrasse)

ACHTUNG!

After **in, neben, hinter, vor, auf, gegenüber**, use:

der	dem
Disco	Kino
Post	Kaufhaus
Bank	Schwimmbad
Apotheke	Museum
Metzgerei	Gemüsehändler
Bäckerei	Supermarkt
Kirche	Marktplatz
Drogerie	
X-straße	

Antworte schriftlich

Use the map above.

1. Wo ist die nächste Drogerie?
2. Wo ist der Gemüsehändler?
3. Wo ist die Post?
4. Wo ist das Kaufhaus?
5. Wo ist die Metzgerei?
6. Wo ist das nächste Museum?
7. Wo ist die nächste Apotheke?
8. Wo ist hier ein Supermarkt?

Kannst du mehr?

Und in deiner Stadt?
Wo sind da die Geschäfte?
Where are the shops in your town? Could you explain to a German-speaking person?

35   Im Lebensmittelgeschäft   35

eine Schachtel eine Flasche eine Dose eine Tüte

ein Pfund ein Kilogramm ein Stück ein Liter

Mache eine Liste

Was kaufst du in einer | Tüte | Dose | Flasche | Schachtel ?
| Chips | Limo | Wein | Pralinen

Ich möchte gern Haben Sie	eine	Tüte Dose Flasche Schachtel	Bonbons Suppe Sprudel Streichhölzer
	ein	Pfund Kilogramm Liter Stück	Käse Bananen Milch Kuchen

Kapiert?

Listen to this shopping list. Write down what you have to buy. There are eight items altogether.

Einkaufen

Hier ist eine Einkaufsliste.
Wo kannst du das kaufen?

Ich kaufe Tomaten im Gemüseladen.
Ich kaufe Käse im ____.

im	in der
Gemüseladen	Apotheke
Supermarkt	Drogerie
Lebensmittelgeschäft	Metzgerei
Kaufhaus	Fleischerei
	Bäckerei

1 Pfund Tomaten
½ Pfund Käse
1 Dose Fisch
½ Pfund Butter
2 Flaschen Limonade
1 Weißbrot
4 Stück Kuchen
1 Pfund Äpfel

Und jetzt du!

Erfinde Dialoge mit deinem Partner.

A kauft ein.

1 Say hello.
3 Ask if they have any tomatoes.
5 Say how much you want.

7 Say no thank you.
   Ask how much it costs.
9 Pay and say goodbye.

B verkauft.

2 Say hello.
4 Say yes.
6 Ask if the customer wants anything else.

8 Say the price.
10 Say thank you and goodbye.

Kannst du mehr?

Make up more dialogues in different shops. Take it in
turns to be the shopkeeper and customer.

Wir machen ein Picknick!

Was habt ihr denn da?

You are going on a picnic with some friends.

1 Ask a number of people in your class what they like to eat and drink.

| Nicht vergessen: Was ißt du gern? |
| Was trinkst du gern? |

2 Make a shopping list.
Decide what kind of containers/quantities you need of each item.
Beispiel: 1 kg Äpfel

3 Write down in which shop you can buy each item.
Beispiel: 1 kg Äpfel – Gemüseladen

4 Make up conversations at the different shops.

36   Im Kaufhaus   36

3. STOCK:	SPORTARTIKEL, ELEKTROGERÄTE, MÖBEL, CAFE
2. STOCK:	HERRENBEKLEIDUNG, KINDERBEKLEIDUNG, SPIELZEUG
1. STOCK:	DAMENBEKLEIDUNG, SCHUHE, LEDERWAREN
ERDGESCHOSS:	KOSMETIK, SCHREIBWAREN, ZEITUNGEN
TIEFPARTERRE:	LEBENSMITTEL, GARTENGERÄTE

Read the notice board above. Where would you buy the following?

1. Shoes?
2. A T-shirt for your little brother?
3. Some perfume for your mother?
4. A record for your friend?
5. A football shirt for your dad?
6. Some postcards to send home?
7. Something to eat on the journey back?

Geschenk

Kassette

Postkarten

Souvenirs

Kette

Schallplatte

Parfum

Pralinen

Sticker

Rasierwasser

Abzeichen

98

Kapiert?

Hör zu! What are they buying
Match the pictures with the text you hear on the tape.
When the pictures are in the right order, what word do they spell?

s	h	u	a
f	u	k	a

	Was?	Wie?
	What you may hear:	
	Can I help you?	Kann ich Ihnen helfen?
	Which size would you like?	Welche Größe möchten Sie?
	Which colour would you like?	Welche Farbe möchten Sie?

Geschenke

Make a list of the members of your family and write down what you could bring each of them back from a holiday in Germany.

Beispiel: Mutti – eine Kette
Opa – eine Flasche Wein

Kannst du mehr?

State what you are buying your family in full sentences.

Beispiel: Ich kaufe eine Kette für Mutti.

ACHTUNG!

After 'ich kaufe' use:
einen with **der** words
eine with **die** words
ein with **das** words

Wiederholung Sieben

◉ Kapiert?

Who buys what for whom? Copy the grid and fill it in.

Wer?	Was?	Für wen?
Matthias		
Kai		
Sonja		
Dirk		
Almut		
Claudia		

🗨 Plappermaul

Wieviele Dialoge kannst du mit einem Partner erfinden? Du hast fünf Minuten.

A ist Verkäufer.
B kauft ein.
(Watch out – not every box fits every dialogue!)

A	Bitte sehr?	Was darf's sein?	Kann ich Ihnen helfen?	Bitte schön?
B	Ich möchte diese Schallplatte.	Haben Sie Sandalen?	Ich möchte einen Pullover.	Ich kaufe diese Kette.
A	Ja sicher. Welche Größe?	Gerne. Das macht DM10.	Aber natürlich. Welche Farbe?	Gerne. Das kostet DM20.

Kannst du Deutsch schreiben?

Make a list of all the shops whose names you know in German. Beside each one, list in German all the things you might buy there.

NOW YOU ARE READY FOR WAYSTAGE 7

37 Schulen in Deutschland 37

Kinder von 3 bis 6

Ein Kindergarten
Gabi geht in den Kindergarten.
Sie ist 4 Jahre alt.

Kinder von 6 bis 10

Eine Grundschule
Anna geht auf die Grundschule.
Sie ist 8 Jahre alt.

Kinder von 10 bis 15

Eine Hauptschule
Jens geht auf die Hauptschule.
Er ist 13 Jahre alt.
Er will später Verkäufer werden.

101

Kinder von 10 bis 16

Eine Realschule
Jürgen geht auf die Realschule.
Er ist 15 Jahre alt.
Er will später Bankbeamter werden.

Kinder von 10 bis 19

Ein Gymnasium
Monika geht auf das Gymnasium.
Sie ist 17 Jahre alt.
Sie will später Physiklehrerin werde

Kinder von 10 bis 15, 16 oder 19

Eine Gesamtschule
Dirk geht auf die Gesamtschule.
Er ist 14 Jahre alt.
Er will später Automechaniker oder
Sportlehrer werden.

Was lernen die Kinder?

- Gabi lernt Singen (Musik)  und Malen (Kunst)

Anna lernt Lesen  und  Schreiben (Deutsch)

Sachkunde    Sport     und Werken

Jens lernt Deutsch    Mathe 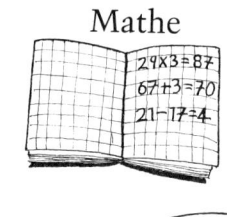    Erdkunde

Naturwissenschaft   Hauswirtschaft    Geschichte und  Englisch

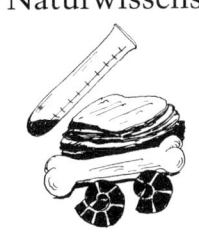

Jürgen lernt auch noch Französisch

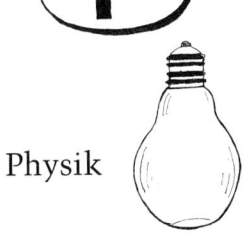

Sozialkunde    Physik   und Biologie

Monika lernt auch noch Chemie

Latein    und Politik

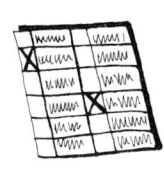

Ich lerne Hauswirtschaft Chemie und Rechnen.

Kapiert?

These children are going to tell you what school they go to and what they study. Copy the grid and as you listen, fill in each person's age and school. Then see if you can catch which subjects he or she has today, and tick them on the grid.

Name	Wie alt?	Schule	Deutsch	Mathe	Englisch	Biologie	Sport
Gregor							
Ines							
Mike							
Nicole							

Kannst du Deutsch schreiben?

Write about the four children from the completed grid.

Beispiel: Gregor ist zwölf. Er hat heute Deutsch, Mathe, Englisch und Sport.

Was?	**Wie?**
ask what school someone attends say what type of school you attend	Auf welche Schule gehst du? Ich gehe auf eine Gesamtschule. Ich gehe auf eine Realschule. Ich gehe auf ein Gymnasium.
ask what lessons someone has today say what lessons you have today	Was hast du heute? Ich habe heute ____ und ____.

Und jetzt du!

Partner A

Pretend to be one of the people on the grid at the top of this page. Answer your partner's questions.

Partner B

Interview your partner.
Find out: his or her name
his or her age
his or her school.

38 — Mein Stundenplan — 38

Hallo! Ich heiße Marika. Ich bin dreizehn Jahre alt und wohne in Dortmund. Das ist in Westdeutschland. Ich gehe auf die Realschule und bin in der siebten Klasse. Meine Klassenlehrerin heißt Frau Jung. Hier ist mein Stundenplan.

STUNDENPLAN	BRAUN Marika			Klasse 7b	
MONTAG	DIENSTAG	MITTWOCH	DONNERSTAG	FREITAG	SAMSTAG
1 8.10–8.55 Biologie	Deutsch	Religion	Geschichte	—	—
2 9.00–9.45 Erdkunde	Mathe	Physik	Deutsch	Mathe	Englisch
ERSTE PAUSE						
3 10.00–10.45 Deutsch	Geschichte	Biologie	Mathe	Erdkunde	Religion
4 10.50–11.35 Mathe	Englisch	Englisch	Physik	Französisch	Französisch
ZWEITE PAUSE						
5 11.55–12.40 Musik	Französisch	Sport	Französisch	Deutsch	—
6 12.45–13.30 —	Musik	Sport	Englisch		

Falsch oder richtig?

1 Marika ist zwölf Jahre alt.
2 Sie wohnt in Regensburg.
3 Das ist in Süddeutschland.
4 Sie geht auf die Gesamtschule.
5 Sie ist in der siebten Klasse.
6 Ihre Klassenlehrerin heißt Frau Bonn.
7 Am Montag hat Marika Mathe.
8 Am Dienstag hat sie Biologie.
9 Am Mittwoch hat sie Französisch.
10 Am Donnerstag hat sie Englisch.
11 Am Freitag hat sie Deutsch.
12 Sie geht auch am Sonntag zur Schule.

Kannst du mehr?

Antworte auf deutsch:
1. Wie alt ist Marika?
2. Wo geht sie zur Schule?
3. Wie heißt ihre Klassenlehrerin?
4. Was hat Marika am Montag um neun Uhr?
5. Was hat sie um zehn Uhr?
6. Und um elf Uhr?
7. Und was hat sie am Montag um zwölf Uhr?

Was?	Wie?
ask when school starts	Wann beginnt die Schule?
ask when school finishes	Wann ist die Schule aus?
say when school starts	Die Schule beginnt um 8 Uhr.
say when school finishes	Die Schule ist um 1 Uhr aus.

Und jetzt du!

Ask your partner what school he or she attends, and what time it starts and finishes. Answer truthfully the first time, and make up an answer as if you went to school in Germany the second time.

Was?	Wie?
ask what someone has in period 1	Was hast du in der ersten Stunde?
ask when someone has a lesson	Wann hast du ____?
say when you have a lesson	Ich habe _____ am Montag.
	Ich habe __ um 10 Uhr.
	Ich habe __ in der ersten Stunde.
say you have a free period	Ich habe nichts.

⊙ Kapiert?

Look at this incomplete timetable. As you listen to the tape, list the subjects which belong in the blank spaces.

NAME:			KLASSE:			
	MONTAG	DIENSTAG	MITTWOCH	DONNERSTAG	FREITAG	SAMSTAG
1.			—	—	Deutsch	—
2.	Mathe	Religion	Sozialkunde	Englisch	Biologie	
3.			Biologie	Erdkunde	Physik	Mathe
4.	Erdkunde	Chemie		Chemie		Religion
5.	—				Sozialkunde	—
6.	—	Mathe	Physik		—	—

Wie ist dein Stundenplan?

Schreib deinen Stundenplan auf deutsch. Frag deinen Lehrer oder deine Lehrerin, wie die Fächer (*subjects*) auf deutsch heißen.

Was?	Wie?
ask the German for a word	Wie heißt ___ auf deutsch?
ask for the spelling	Wie schreibt man das?

🗣 Und jetzt du!

Frag deinen Partner/deine Partnerin, was er/sie in der Schule hat. Antworte.

Beispiel:
Was hast du am Montag in der dritten Stunde? — Ich habe Mathe.
Wann hast du Deutsch? — Am Montag und Donnerstag.

✂ Kannst du mehr?

Partner **A** is Marika. Your timetable is on page 105.
Partner **B** is Hans. Your timetable is at the top of this page. It is incomplete, but all your free periods are marked.

Speaking only in German, work out when you can meet next week.
'When shall we meet?' = '**Wann treffen wir uns?**'

39 — Was ist dein Lieblingsfach? — 39

Ich heiße Volker Schlosser und bin 12 Jahre alt. Ich komme aus Betzdorf in Deutschland und gehe auf das Gymnasium. Ich mag Mathematik und Physik gern. Physik ist sehr interessant.

Mein Name ist Sandra Greb. Ich bin 11 Jahre alt und wohne in Wien, in Österreich. In der Schule mag ich Englisch und Deutsch gern. Englisch ist leicht and macht Spaß.

Ich bin 13 Jahre alt und heiße Jörg Kemper. Ich komme aus Leipzig in Ostdeutschland. Ich gehe auf das Gymnasium. Russisch und Geschichte sind meine Lieblingsfächer. Ich finde Mathematik langweilig.

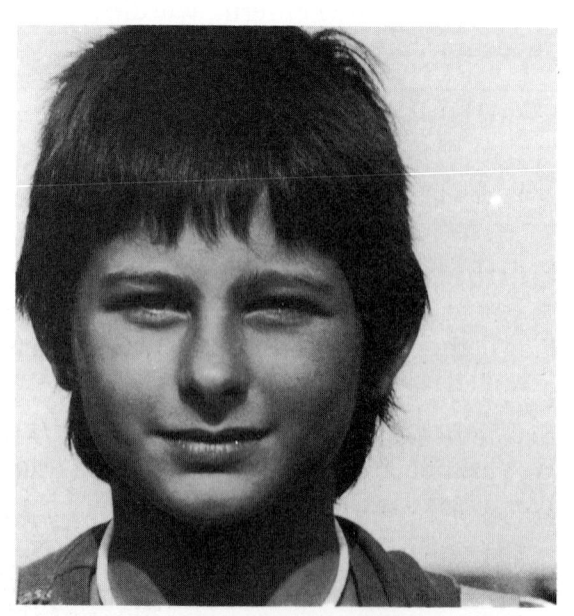

Grützi! Ich heiße Maria Bernardsgrütter und wohne in Bern, in der Schweiz. Ich bin 12. In der Schule mag ich Kunst und Sport besonders gern. Ich finde Englisch schwer.

Kapiert?

Wer mag was? Copy the grid and put ticks and crosses to show which subjects the pupils like and dislike.

Name	Englisch	Sport	Mathe	Deutsch	Physik	Kunst
Ulrike						
Axel						
Maren						
Frank						
Barbara						

	Was?	**Wie?**
	ask what someone likes	Was magst du gern? Magst du Englisch?
	say what you like	Ich mag ⎯⎯ ∣ (gern). ∣ sehr gern. ∣ ganz gern.
	say what you dislike	Ich mag ⎯⎯ ∣ nicht (gern). ∣ gar nicht (gern).
	say what you enjoy	⎯⎯ macht Spaß.
	ask someone's opinion of a subject	Wie findest du ⎯⎯?
	give your opinion of a subject	Ich finde ⎯⎯ ∣ leicht. ∣ schwer. ∣ interessant. ∣ langweilig. ∣ einfach Klasse!

Gruppenarbeit

Conduct a class survey in German. Ask four or five people what they think of different subjects. Complete a chart like the one above to record their replies. Use these abbreviations:

LEI – leicht
SCH – schwer
INT – interessant
LAN – langweilig
E.K. – einfach Klasse

40 — Was ist dein Hobby? — 40

Mein Hobby ist lesen.

Mein Hobby ist Briefmarken sammeln.

Mein Hobby ist radfahren

Mein Hobby ist Platten hören.

Mein Hobby ist fernsehen.

Mein Hobby ist kochen.

Mein Hobby ist basteln.

Mein Hobby ist stricken.

Mein Hobby ist malen.

Mein Hobby ist angeln.

Mein Hobby ist fotografieren.

Mein Hobby ist tanzen.

Wieviele Hobbys kannst du finden?

```
C H L N A S Z O P A T X W G L E J N B I
O G O Z G W B N E Z L A A B K B K U Z P
N D J H A L P H U P T B G M O E Y S K X
T F S S F W X E M O W P S Z C R T W C D
T Q K B O E T K X B U L T D H L A K A P
X A S L P Y C U E S S E N T E F Y C H V
K E B A S R G J Q O W T E N N I S R P R
S C H W I M M E N D W I B T A N Z E N Q
Q S T R I C K E N O Z V A F R S W S F L
R K Z F S C H A L L P L A T T E N B X C
A V F F O T O G R A F I E R E N J K H L
D B E D K W Q S E H D A N G E L N P G J
F F R H H R Y A F B A S T E L N T J Z F
A I N V S H X U L B A D M I N T O N E R
H L S M A L E N X Z E I C H N E N H B Z
R M E C F J H K Q B D L D Z P S Y L Z A
E E H G E O F U S S B A L L F O V V E Q
N Z E S T W C E S U T R I N K E N S W C
Y L N B R I E F M A R K E N Q E S R W H
T Q L U U J A H M V K M N L E S E N E E
```

☻ Kapiert?

Welche Hobbys haben diese Kinder?
1. Simones Hobby ist ____.
2. Manuels Hobby ist ____.
3. Kirstins Hobbys sind ____ und ____.
4. Paolos Hobby ist ____.
5. Sorayas Hobby ist ____.
6. Ralfs Hobby ist ____.

Was?	**Wie?**
ask if someone has a hobby	Hast du ein Hobby?
answer	Ja, angeln.
	Ja, mein Hobby ist angeln.
	Nein, ich habe kein Hobby.
ask what someone's hobby is	Was ist dein Hobby?

Gruppenarbeit

Conduct a class survey, to find out about people's hobbies. Start with your neighbours. Record your answers in German on a chart like this.

	Name	Hobby/s
1		
2		
3		
4		
5		

Meine Hobbys sind essen, trinken und schlafen.

Now write the information down in sentences.

41 — Was kannst du machen? — 41

Ich kann auf Stelzen laufen, aber nicht sehr gut!

Ich kann Kanu fahren. Ich bin in einem Klub.

Ich kann Frisbee spielen, aber mein Bruder will nicht spielen.

Ich kann radfahren. Mein Cousin kann Motorrad fahren.

Ich kann nicht laufen!
Mein Bein ist gebrochen.

Und du? Say which of these activities you can or cannot do.

Kapiert?

Was kann Bernd machen?

1. speak German
2. speak English
3. ride a horse
4. ride a motorbike
5. play football
6. canoe
7. play frisbee
8. walk on stilts
9. ride a bicycle
10. swim

√ = kann

× = kann nicht

? = ich weiß nicht

Was?	Wie?
ask if someone can do something	Kannst du schwimmen?
say what you can do	Ich kann reiten.
say what a friend can do	Peter kann kochen.
say what a friend cannot do	Barbara kann nicht stricken.
say how well you can do something	Ich kann gut | kochen. sehr gut ganz gut nicht gut nicht sehr gut

Und jetzt du!

Interview your partner. Find out:

– his or her name
– his or her age
– where he or she is from
– what school he or she attends
– what lessons he or she has today
– what hobby or hobbies he or she has
– if he or she can swim, ride, or cook.

Kannst du mehr?

Write a letter to a German pen-friend. Tell him or her about your hobbies. Ask about his or hers.

Wiederholung Acht

> Jena, den 8. Oktober
>
> Lieber Jens,
> Wie geht's? Ich wohne jetzt in Jena. Das ist im Süden von der DDR. Meine neue Adresse ist:
> Marienweg 14
> DDR 6900 Jena
> Ich gehe hier auf die Oberschule. Die ist ganz neu, und Schüler und Lehrer sind sehr freundlich. Mein Klassenlehrer ist Herr Becker und die Direktorin heißt Schmidt. Ich lerne Deutsch, Mathe, Russisch, Erdkunde, Geschichte, Physik, Biologie, Kunst, Politik und Sport. Biologie ist mein Lieblingsfach. Das ist sehr interessant und macht Spaß. Ich mag auch Erdkunde und Deutsch. Mein Deutschlehrer ist sehr nett. Er heißt Meyer und ist mein Lieblingslehrer. Deutsch habe ich fünfmal in der Woche, aber Erdkunde nur zweimal, am Dienstag und am Freitag. Sport macht natürlich auch Spaß, aber ich finde Kunst und Geschichte langweilig. Mathematik mag ich nicht gern.
> Wie ist Deine Schule? Schreib bald wieder!
>
> Dein Axel
>
> P.S.: Ich habe ein neues Hobby – Briefmarken sammeln.

Antworte auf englisch

1 Who is Axel's form teacher?
2 What is the head's name?
3 What is Axel's favourite subject?
4 Why?
5 What else does he like?
6 Who is his favourite teacher?
7 Why?
8 What does Axel not like at school?
9 What does he find boring?
10 What is his new hobby?

Das ist neu:

der Schüler	pupil
der Direktorin	headmistress
freundlich	friendly

Kannst du mehr?

Antworte auf deutsch:

1 Wo wohnt Axel?
2 Wo ist das?
3 Auf welche Schule geht Axel?
4 Wie heißt die Direktorin?
5 Was findet Axel interessant?
6 Was mag er nicht gern?

NOW YOU ARE READY FOR WAYSTAGE 8.

42 — Das ist mein Haus — 42

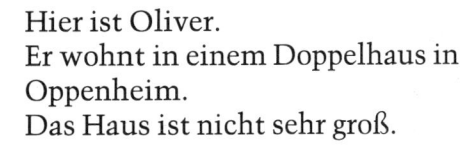

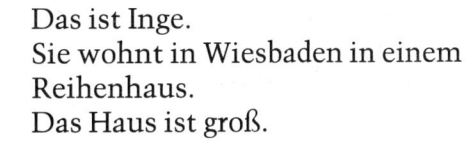

Hier ist Oliver.
Er wohnt in einem Doppelhaus in Oppenheim.
Das Haus ist nicht sehr groß.

Das ist Inge.
Sie wohnt in Wiesbaden in einem Reihenhaus.
Das Haus ist groß.

Das da ist Natascha.
Sie wohnt in einem Einfamilienhaus.
Das ist in Rostock und ziemlich klein.

Und hier ist Giorgio.
Er wohnt in Wien in einer Wohnung.
Giorgios Wohnung ist sehr groß.

Giorgios Wohnung

Listen to the tape and look at the plan of Giorgio's flat. Can you find your way around?

Hier ist ein Plan von Giorgios Wohnung.

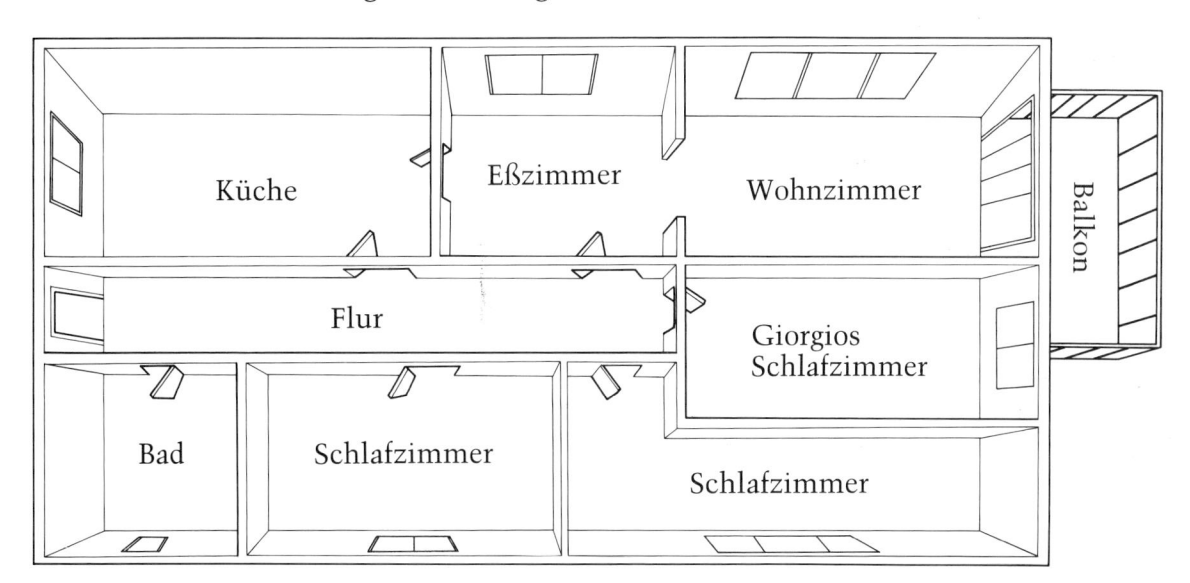

Küche	Eßzimmer	Wohnzimmer	Balkon
Flur		Giorgios Schlafzimmer	
Bad	Schlafzimmer	Schlafzimmer	

115

Kapiert?

a Olivers Haus
Richtig oder falsch?
1 Olivers Haus hat vier Zimmer, Küche und Bad.
2 Oliver hat zwei Schlafzimmer.
3 Das Eßzimmer ist im Erdgeschoß.
4 Olivers Zimmer ist neben dem Bad.

b Inges Haus
Answer these questions in English:
1 How many rooms are there altogether?
2 How many bedrooms are there?
3 Which rooms are downstairs?
4 Which rooms are upstairs?

c Das ist Nataschas Haus
Listen to what Natascha has to say. She is speaking very slowly. Draw a plan of her house.

ein Doppelhaus

ein Reihenhaus

ein Einfamilienhaus

ein Wohnblock mit vielen Wohnungen

Und dein Haus?

Zeichne einen Plan und schreibe die Namen der Zimmer auf deutsch.
Draw a plan of your house and label it in German.
Zuerst das Erdgeschoß.
Dann der erste Stock.

Ergänze diesen Text:

Ich heiße _____.
Ich wohne in _____ in einem Haus/in einer Wohnung.
Mein Haus/Meine Wohnung ist _____ _____.
Mein Haus/Meine Wohnung hat _____ Zimmer, Küche und Bad.
Im Erdgeschoß sind _____.
Im ersten Stock sind _____.

Die Möbel

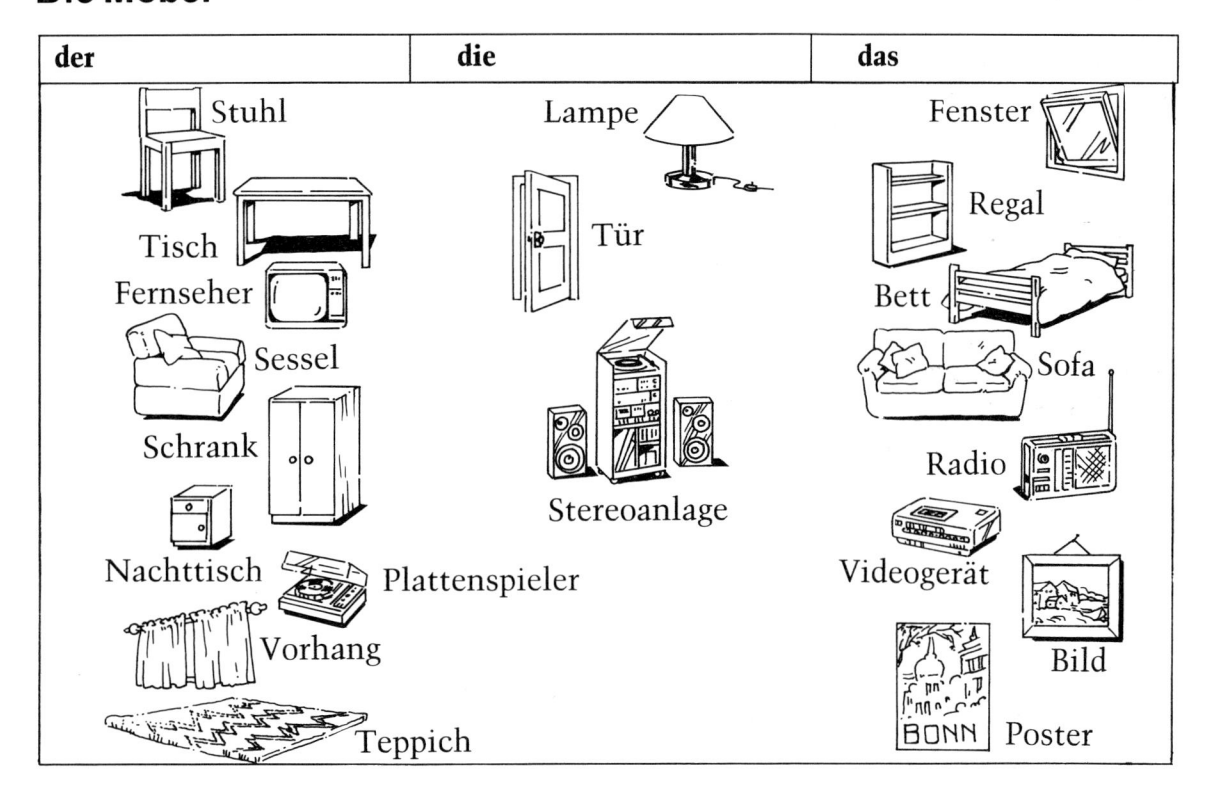

der	die	das

- Stuhl
- Tisch
- Fernseher
- Sessel
- Schrank
- Nachttisch
- Plattenspieler
- Vorhang
- Teppich

- Lampe
- Tür
- Stereoanlage

- Fenster
- Regal
- Bett
- Sofa
- Radio
- Videogerät
- Bild
- Poster

Das ist Nataschas Zimmer.

Was hat Tascha?
Tascha hat einen Kleiderschrank.

Was hat Tascha nicht?
Tascha hat keine Stereoanlage.
Und du? Was ist in deinem Zimmer?

Das ist Olivers Zimmer.

Was hat Oliver?
Oliver hat einen Fernseher.

Was hat Oliver nicht?
Oliver hat keinen Plattenspieler.

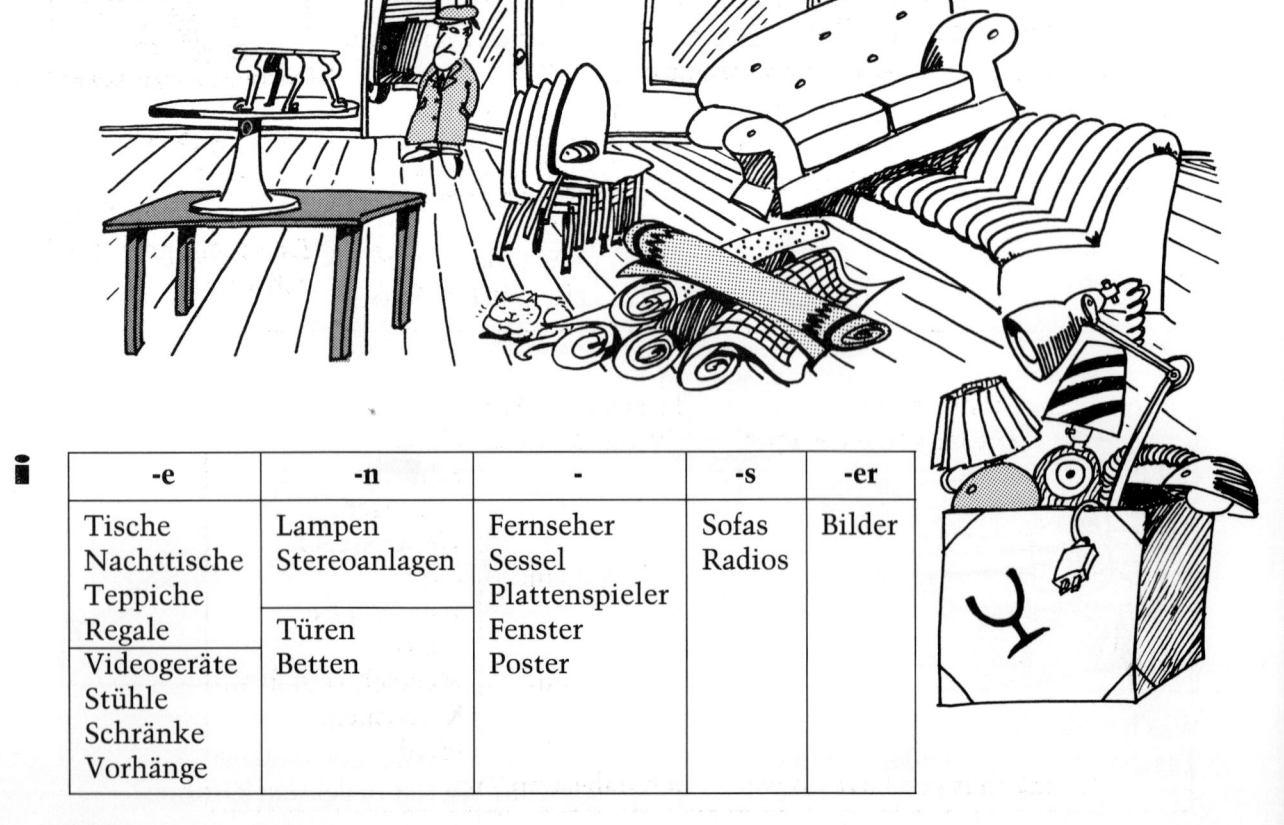

Plurals

-e	-n	-	-s	-er
Tische	Lampen	Fernseher	Sofas	Bilder
Nachttische	Stereoanlagen	Sessel	Radios	
Teppiche		Plattenspieler		
Regale	Türen	Fenster		
Videogeräte	Betten	Poster		
Stühle				
Schränke				
Vorhänge				

118

43 — Meine Tiere — 43

Hallo. Ich bin der Frank aus Freiburg und hier ist mein Hund.
Er ist klein.
Sein Fell (Haar) ist kurz und hellbraun.
Er ist sechs Jahre alt und heißt Jakob.

Meine Freundin Ulla hat einen Hamster.
Er heißt Otto.
Er ist sieben Monate alt und ganz klein.
Er ist braun.

Sie hat auch ein Kaninchen.
Es heißt Schneewittchen.
Es ist weiß.
Sein Fell ist lang und seine Augen sind rot.

In meiner Klasse haben viele Tiere.
Jutta hat einen Wellensittich.

Christof hat eine Katze und zwei Goldfische.

Paulo hat zwei Meerschweinchen.

Fatima hat eine Wüstenratte und eine weiße Maus.

Und Udo hat sogar ein Pferd.
Das heißt Wildfang.
Es ist sehr groß und schwarz.

Was?	**Wie?**
ask someone if he or she has a pet	Hast du ein Tier?
say that you have a pet	Ich habe einen Hund. / Hamster. / Goldfisch. / Wellensittich.
	eine Katze. / Wüstenratte. / Maus.
	ein Meerschweinchen. / Kaninchen. / Pferd.
say that you have no pet	Ich habe kein Tier.

Kapiert?

Hör zu!
Match the people on the left with the animals on the right after listening to the tape.

Plurals

–e	–n	–
Hunde Wellensittiche Goldfische Pferde Mäuse	Wüstenratten	Hamster Meerschweinchen Kaninchen

Gruppenarbeit

Ask your partner if he or she has a pet.
Make a list for the class.

Tiere	Hunde	Katzen	Hamster	Wellensittiche	Mäuse
Jason	–	1	zwei	–	–
Carol	–	zwei	–	–	1

Kannst du mehr?

Write a report about the animals owned by members of your class.

Beispiel: Wir haben sechzehn Hunde, zwei Katzen, drei Wellensittiche, ...

Oder:
Fünf Personen haben einen Hund.
Zwei Personen haben kein Tier.

Oder:
Jason hat einen Hund und zwei Hamster.
Carol hat zwei Katzen und eine Maus.

Was oder wen magst du? ♥ ♥ ♥?

Magst du ...

Hunde?	Ja!	Ich mag Hunde sehr gern ♥ ♥ ♥
Katzen?		gern ♥ ♥
Kaninchen?		ganz gern ♥
Wüstenratten	Nein!	nicht gern ✗
Mäuse		gar nicht gern ✗ ✗

Was mag dein Partner oder deine Partnerin?
Was mag deine Lehrerin oder dein Lehrer?
Frag mal. Was ist das populärste Tier in deiner Klasse? Und in deiner Familie?

Kapiert?

Listen to these ten people. They are telling you which animals they like or don't like. Copy the grid into your exercise book and mark it with a plus sign for each one they like and a minus sign for each one they don't like.

Name	Hunde	Wellensittiche	Goldfische	Katzen	Hamster	Kaninchen
Uschi						
Frank						
Jürgen						
Christiane						
Hajo						
Sonja						
Mischa						
Monika						
Paulo						
Fatima						

Und jetzt du!

How many questions can you and your partner ask each other about which animals you like in one minute? You must ask and answer the questions in German.
Auf die Plätze, fertig, los!

44 Wie sieht der denn aus? 44

Sie ist groß.    Er ist mittelgroß.    Ich bin ganz klein.

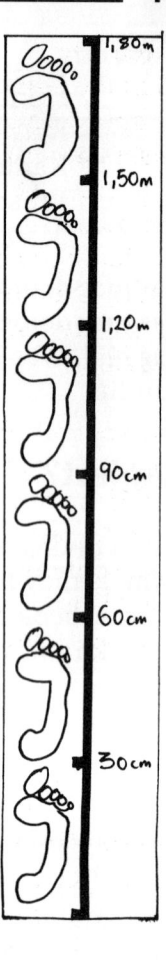

Er ist dick.    Sie ist schlank.    Ich bin vollschlank.

Sein Haar ist lockig.    Ihr Haar ist lang.    Mein Haar ist kurz.

die Augen    Er hat eine Brille auf. 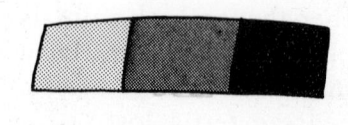   hell   mittel   dunkel

Oliver

Guten Tag.
Ich heiße Oliver Fränkel.
Ich bin 13 und ich komme aus
Kaiserslautern. Ich bin 1,62 m groß.
Mein Haar ist blond und meine Augen
sind blau.
Auf dem Foto hier bin ich mit meinem
Bruder Thorsten.
Ich bin rechts. Ich habe ein T-Shirt und
Jeans an.

Thorsten ist 16.
Er ist 1,75 m groß.
Sein Haar ist mittelblond.
Seine Augen sind grün.
Er ist schlank.
Er hat Jeans, ein T-Shirt und eine
Lederjacke an.

Hier ist meine Freundin.
Sie heißt Karin. Sie ist zwölf Jahre alt.
Ihr Haar ist braun und kurz.
Ihre Augen sind braun.
Sie ist mittelgroß und schlank.
Sie hat ein T-Shirt und Bermudashorts
an.

Was?	Wie?
ask someone to describe: – a boy/man – a girl woman – him or herself	Wie sieht er aus? Wie sieht sie aus? Wie siehst du aus?
describe a man/boy: – his height – his build – his hair – his eyes	Er ist 1,90 m groß. Er ist nicht sehr schlank. Sein Haar ist blond und lang. Seine Augen sind grau.
describe a girl/woman – her height – her build – her hair – her eyes	Sie ist mittelgroß. Sie ist ziemlich schlank. Ihr Haar ist rot und kurz. Ihre Augen sind grün.

Was?	Wie?
describe yourself	
– your height	Ich bin klein.
– your build	Ich bin vollschlank.
– your hair	Mein Haar ist mittelbraun und lockig.
– your eyes	Meine Augen sind grünbraun.

Kapiert?

Junge oder Mädchen?

a Listen to the following descriptions very carefully. For each one, decide whether it is about a boy or a girl. Copy the grid and put a tick in the correct column for each item. There will be ten altogether.

	Junge	Mädchen
1		
2		
3		
4		
5		
6		
7		
8		
9		
10		

b One of the two girls in the photograph above has been observed shoplifting. Listen to the description and decide which one.

c Listen to the descriptions of the following two people. Can you draw an identikit picture of each of them?

Kannst du mehr?

Bring some photographs of friends or members of your family and reply to Tanja's letter (opposite), describing the people in the photographs.

Und jetzt du!

1 Describe another person in the class or one of your teachers to your partner and let him or her guess whom you are describing.
2 Play ten questions. Think of a person. Your partner asks you questions in German, e.g. **Ist er groß?**
You can only answer **ja** or **nein**. Your partner has to guess who the person is in ten questions or less.
3 Describe a person for your partner to draw.

Ein Brief von Tanja

Unfortunately Tanja forgot to label the photographs she sent with her letter. Read it carefully and see if you can identify the people in each picture.
Write your answers in your exercise books.

Beispiel: Auf Bild zwei ist Tanjas Bruder.

Mainz, den 12. Juli

Liebe Jane,

Hier sind fünf Fotos von meiner Familie und Freunden. Die Fotos habe ich im Schwimmbad und beim Einkaufen gemacht.

Auf dem ersten Bild ist meine Freundin im Schwimmbad. Sie heißt Heike und ist sehr nett. Wie Du siehst, ist ihr Haar kurz und braun und sie ist nicht sehr schlank.
Der kleine Junge im Schwimmbad ist mein Bruder Paul. Er ist erst acht und ganz schön frech. Auf dem Foto ist er sehr braun und sein Haar ist hellblond. Normalerweise ist es mittelblond.

Auf dem dritten Bild siehst Du mich und meine Oma beim Einkaufen. Omas Haar ist kurz und lockig. Sie hat eine Brille auf. Mein Haar ist jetzt schon ganz lang. Auf dem vierten Bild sind Mutti, Vati und Sabine. Mutti ist sehr groß (1,78 m) und schlank. Sabines Haar ist kurz und braun. Vati hat nicht viel Haar. Es ist mittelblond wie Pauls.

Auf dem letzten Bild ist mein Opa mit meiner Tante und Kusine. Opa ist ziemlich klein, sein Haar ist weiß und er hat eine Brille. Er ist 62 Jahre alt. Andrea, meine Kusine, hat kurzes braunes Haar. Sie ißt gerade ein Eis. Meine Tante Brigitte ist Vatis Schwester. Sie ist 32. Sie hat ein T-Shirt und einen Rock an.

Hast Du Fotos von Deiner Familie? Bitte sende mir ein paar.
Bis bald!
Schöne Grüße
Tanja

45 — Wie man Tiere beschreibt — 45

Ich habe **einen** Hund.
Mein Hund heißt Hasso.
Er ist neun Jahre alt.
Sein Fell ist lockig.
Er ist weiß, schwarz und braun.

Ich habe **eine** Katze.
Meine Katze heißt Muschi.
Sie ist vier Jahre alt.
Ihr Fell ist kurz.
Sie ist grau.

Ich habe **ein** Kaninchen.
Mein Kaninchen heißt Hasi.
Es ist fünfzehn Monate alt.
Sein Fell ist lang.
Es ist braun.

Kapiert?

Listen to these boys and girls describing their animals.
Copy the grid and fill it in.

	Tier	Alter	Farbe	Andere Information
1				
2				
3				
4				
5				

Kannst du Deutsch lesen?

Lieber Jason,

ja, ich mag Katzen sehr gern. Aber wir haben keine. Meine Mutter sagt, es ist nicht hygienisch in einer Bäckerei. Ich habe einen Wellensittich. Er heißt Hansi. Er ist grün und gelb. Er kann prima singen.

Schöne Grüße

Andreas

1 What does Andreas think of cats?
2 Why can't he have one?
3 What pet has he got?
4 What is it like?

Welches Tier?

Look at the pictures of these animals. There are twenty-five sentences to describe them, five for each animal. Which sentences go with which picture?

Meine Katze heißt Muschi.
Ich habe ein Pferd.
Es ist weiß.
Er ist blau und grün.
Sein Fell ist kurz.
Er ist schwarz, grau und weiß.
Ich habe eine Katze.
Er ist sehr klein.
Muschi ist mittelgroß.
Er kann gut singen.
Sein Fell ist lang.
Blanko ist sehr groß.
Rocko ist vier Jahre alt.
Er ist ein Jahr alt.
Mein Hamster heißt Andie.
Ich habe einen Hund.
Ihr Fell ist grau und weiß.
Mein Pferd heißt Blanko.
Sie ist fünf Jahre alt.
Sein Fell ist braun.
Ich habe einen Hamster.
Mein Wellensittich heißt Olli.
Mein Hund heißt Rocko.
Ich habe einen Wellensittich.
Er ist nicht sehr groß.

Und jetzt du!

1 Ask your partner about the animals in the pictures on page 119. If you are answering, make your descriptions as detailed as possible.
2 Play ten questions. Think of an animal. Your partner asks you questions. You are only allowed to answer **Ja** or **Nein**.
3 Ask about and describe your own animals to each other.

Wiederholung Neun

Uwe ist vierzehn und kommt aus Mainz am Rhein. Er wohnt mit seinem Vater und seinem Bruder in einer Wohnung in der Ottostraße. Seine Wohnung ist im zweiten Stock in einem Wohnblock. Sie ist nicht sehr groß – nur zwei Schlafzimmer, ein Wohnzimmer, Küche und Bad. Uwe und sein Bruder haben ein Zimmer mit zwei Betten, einem Kleiderschrank, einem Tisch und vielen Posters. Uwes Hobbys sind basteln und radfahren. Er mag Tiere sehr gern, und möchte einen Hund haben. Aber die Wohnung ist zu klein. Er hat nur einen Hamster, Rosa. Rosa ist vier Monate alt und ganz klein. Uwes Kusine, Bettina, hat ein Pferd und Uwe geht mit Bettina reiten. Das macht Spaß! Das Pferd heißt Flicka und ist schwarz und weiß.

Antworte auf englisch

1. Who does Uwe live with?
2. What street do they live on?
3. What sort of house do they have?
4. How big is it?
5. What is there in Uwe's room?
6. What are Uwe's hobbies?
7. Does he like animals?
8. Describe his pet.
9. Who is Bettina?
10. Describe her pet.

Und jetzt du!

Describe these people to your partner in German, without mentioning the name of the person concerned. Can your partner work out who you mean?

Kannst du mehr?

Now see if you can write a short description of each child.

NOW YOU ARE READY FOR WAYSTAGE 9.

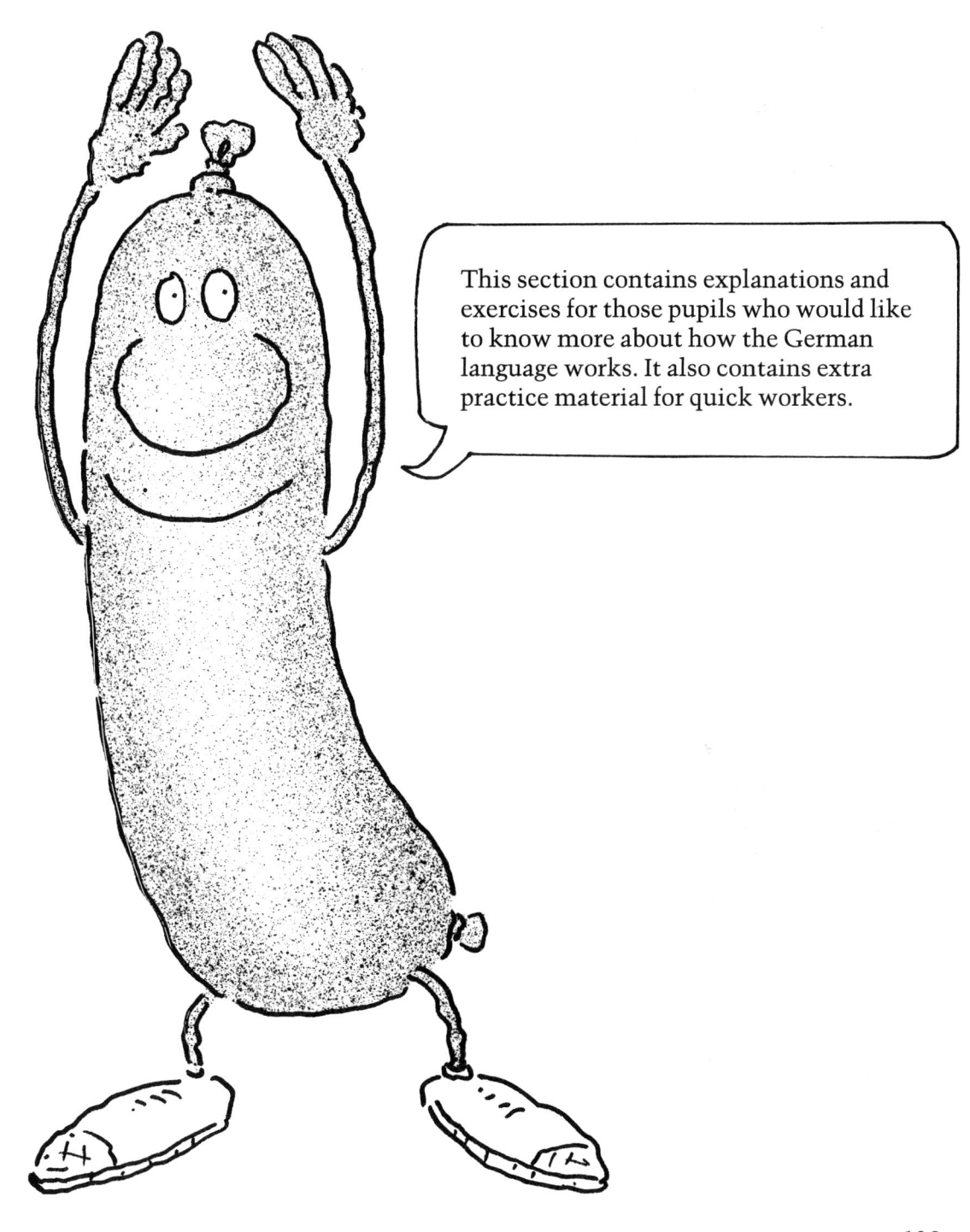

Extension Work

This section contains explanations and exercises for those pupils who would like to know more about how the German language works. It also contains extra practice material for quick workers.

Extension One
Units 1–5

The most important words in any language are *nouns* (words that give things names), *verbs* (words that say what someone is doing), and *adjectives* (words that describe people and things).

When you first learnt to talk, you said nouns first. Maybe your first words were 'Mama', 'Dada', or 'doggy'. Ask your parents if they remember what your first words were.

Then you probably started using verbs like 'give', 'look', 'sleep', and adjectives like 'hot', 'nice', and 'naughty'.

In Book 1 of **Einfach Klasse!**, you can learn about verbs and nouns in German. You can learn about adjectives in Book 2. You may find these sections on grammar quite hard to understand. If so, don't worry – you learnt perfectly good English without knowing about grammar, so there is no reason why you should not learn German too. Lots of German children don't understand grammar, but they still speak perfect German. However, if you can understand these explanations and remember them when you are talking or writing German, you will learn to speak good German more quickly. If you want to take examinations in German when you are older, you will do better if you understand the grammar.

Verbs

Verbs are also called *doing words*. They tell us what people are or what they are doing. Here are some examples:

    to do
    to be
    to live
    to think
    to work

Any one verb can have many different forms. For example:

to think | I *am thinking*!
         | my Mum *thinks* ...
         | you *thought* ...
         | *did* he *think* ... ?

If you want to find an English verb in a dictionary, you must look up what is called the *infinitive* form. That is the part that comes after the word *to*:
   to *eat*, to *dress*, to *go*, to *have*

German verbs have an infinitive form, too, and this is the one you find in the dictionary, or in a vocabulary list like the one at the end of this book. The infinitive nearly always ends in the letters **-en**:

   wohn**en** – to live
   heiß**en** – to be called
   geh**en** – to go
   komm**en** – to come

Aufgabe Eins (Exercise One)

Give yourself five minutes and see how many verbs you can copy down from the vocabulary list at the back of this book. Write the German verb and its English meaning next to each other.

Now you know a little about the infinitive form of German verbs. However, when you use a verb in a sentence, you do not usually want this infinitive form. You generally have to change the ending. In other words, you take off the last letters (**–en**) and put on different letters. Look at these sentences:

Ich komme	aus Nierstein.
Du kommst	aus Belfast.
Er kommt	aus Österreich.
Sie kommt	aus Köln.
Jan kommt	aus Siegen.

| Ich | heiße Anne. |
| Du | heißt Sean. |

130

> Er heißt Bruno.
> Sie heißt Sabine.
> Mein Freund heißt Klaus.

Nearly all verbs have these endings in the *present tense*, that is when you are talking about something which is happening now:

> with **ich** (meaning *I*) use the ending **–e**
> with **du** (meaning *you*) use the ending **–st**
> with **er** (meaning *he*) use the ending **–t**
> with **sie** (meaning *she*) use the ending **–t**
> with a name use the ending **–t**

Which endings are all the same?

> **ACHTUNG!**
>
> You cannot put **sss** or **ßs** in a German verb. If the verb ends in **–sen** or **–ßen**, like **heißen**, and you want the correct form to go with **du**, just add **–t** instead of **–st**.
>
> **du heiß + t = heißt**

Aufgabe Zwei

Complete these sentences by putting the correct ending on the verbs. The **–en** of the infinitive has been taken off already. You should be able to work out what all the sentences mean. If you don't understand a word, look it up at the back.

1 Ich komm___ aus München.
2 Er heiß___ Otto.
3 Woher komm___ du?
4 Mein Freund heiß___ Jan.
5 Wie heiß___ du? (ACHTUNG!)
6 Ich heiß___ Katrin.
7 Woher komm___ er?
8 Hans komm___ aus Berlin.
9 Anna komm___ aus Wien.
10 Wie heiß___ deine Freundin?

Aufgabe Drei

Complete the next set of sentences in the same way. This time the verb is given in brackets at the end of the sentences in its infinitive form. Take off the **–en**, put on the correct ending, and move it to the gap in the sentence.

Beispiel: Ich ___ aus München. (**kommen**)
You write: Ich **komme** aus München.

1 Klaus ___ aus Trier. (**kommen**)
2 Gaby ___ aus Münster. (**kommen**)
3 Ich ___ aus York. (**kommen**)
4 Ich ___ Paul. (**heißen**)
5 Wie ___ du? (**heißen**)
6 Meine Freundin ___ Susy. (**heißen**)
7 Woher ___ Susy? (**kommen**)
8 Du ___ aus Aberdeen, Isobel? (**kommen**)
9 ___ du Peter? (**heißen**)
10 Mein Freund Karl ___ aus Freiburg. (**kommen**)

Aufgabe Vier

It is usually quite easy to remember about verb endings when you are doing a special exercise on them, but can you remember when you are talking or writing normally? If you have a partner working with you, do this exercise orally (aloud). If you are working alone, do it in writing.

Do the following in German:

1 Give your name.
2 Ask your partner's name.
3 Ask your partner the name of a boy in the class.
4 Ask your partner the name of a girl in the class.
5 Ask your partner the teacher's name.
6 Ask your partner his or her friend's name.
7 Ask where your partner comes from.
8 Say where you come from.
9 Ask your partner where the teacher comes from.
10 Ask your partner where his or her friend comes from.

Aufgabe Fünf

Kannst du korrektes Deutsch schreiben?
Can you write correct German?
Look back at Gabi's postcard on page 14 of this book. Can you write a similar card to a German girl? Imagine you have just moved house. Say where you are now, and give your new address. Address the card to Miss Sabine Liebelt, who lives at number 22, Beethovenstraße in Hannover. The postcode for Hannover is 3000. In Germany everyone who lives in the same town has the same postcode.

If you have time, you could write another card to a boy. Instead of **liebe**, use **lieber** to mean *dear*. The word for 'Mr' is **Herr**.

Extension Two
Unit 6

Nouns

Nouns are also called *naming words*. They are the names of people, living things and objects:
 a boy
 a cat
 a tree
 a pen

In German, all nouns begin with a *capital letter*, even in the middle of a sentence:
 ein Kuli
 ein Tisch
 eine Tür

To help you remember when to use a capital letter, remember that if you can touch something, it must be a noun. You can always put the word *the* in front of a noun even when it is on its own:
 the girl
 the window
 the jumper
 the air

Aufgabe Eins

Which of these are nouns?

girl	food	red	sees
car	beetles	eat	bus
drank	cup	sky	little

Can you make a list of the nouns in this paragraph? You may like to try to make another list of the verbs.

> My friend hates school. She doesn't like the teachers, she thinks the work is boring and she thinks the classrooms are like prisons.

> She doesn't go to the same school as me. My school's all right, except that it could do with a coat of paint and some of the teachers are a bit strict. We do lots of different subjects, and we've got nice spacious rooms with plenty of posters and displays. At her school, they only do boring lessons and they never have any discussions. She's going to try and get a transfer.

Gender

German nouns have *gender*. This means that every noun is masculine, feminine or neuter. Sometimes you can guess which it is going to be:

der Mann	*man*	masculine
der Hahn	*cockerel*	
die Frau	*woman*	feminine
die Henne	*hen*	
das Baby	*baby*	neuter
das Küken	*chick*	

Usually, though, you cannot guess the gender of a noun:

der Tisch	*table*	masculine
die Lampe	*light*	feminine
das Buch	*book*	neuter

Occasionally, you would almost certainly be wrong if you guessed:

| das Mädchen | *girl* | neuter |

It is best not to guess. The only way of being sure if a word is masculine, feminine, or neuter is either to look it up, or to learn the gender when you learn the word. You can do this by learning the noun plus the word for 'the' which goes with it:

der Tisch – masculine
die Tasche – feminine
das Buch – neuter.

Aufgabe Zwei

Look these words up in the vocabulary at the back of this book. Work out if each word is masculine, feminine, or neuter by looking at the word for 'the' which is printed in front of it in the vocabulary.

Remember:
  der words are masculine
  die words are feminine
  das words are neuter

Write your findings like this:

1 ein Bleistift – der Bleistift – masculine

1 ein Bleistift
2 eine Tafel
3 ein Tisch
4 eine Tür
5 ein Poster
6 ein Stuhl
7 eine Lampe
8 ein Lineal
9 ein Kuli
10 ein Schrank
11 ein Radiergummi
12 ein Heft
13 ein Buch
14 eine Tasche
15 ein Bild

Have you noticed that the word for 'a' changes?
When is it **ein**?
When is it **eine**?

Ein and eine

You put **eine** with feminine words. It means 'a' or 'an'.

> **eine** Lampe
> **eine** Tasche
> **eine** Tafel

You put **ein** with masculine words and neuter words.

> **ein** Tisch
> **ein** Stuhl
> **ein** Kuli

> **ein** Poster
> **ein** Buch
> **ein** Lineal

Aufgabe Drei

Make a list of all the feminine words in this box. Then look up some more in the vocabulary and add them to your list, putting **eine** in front of each one instead of **die**.

> ein Buch   ein Baby
> eine Lehrerin   ein Tisch
> eine Lampe   eine Jacke
> eine Tasche   eine Tür
> eine Schülerin
> ein Lineal   ein Schrank
> eine Hose   eine Mütze

Aufgabe Vier

Look at this photograph of Karin's class. Can you describe the scene in simple German in your own words? You could start like this:

> Auf dem Foto sind eine Tafel, ein Schrank, ____ und ____.

Mine and thine

If a word is *feminine*, these are the words for:

> a – **eine**
> not a – **keine**
> my – **meine**
> your – **deine**

If a word is *masculine* or *neuter*, these are the words for:

> a – **ein**
> not a – **kein**
> my – **mein**
> your – **dein**

Aufgabe Fünf

The endings have got smudged on some words. Can you rewrite the passage so that all the words are clear? Petra and Jörg are arguing about who owns what!

Petra: He, du! Das ist mei● Tisch!

Jörg: Was?! Ich sitze hier. Das ist mei● Tisch.

Petra: Ach, Quatsch, Mensch! Das ist doch schon immer mei⬛ Tisch gewesen.

Jörg: Ich sage dir, das ist nicht dei⬛ Tisch. Ich bin hier.

Petra: Na was! Ich werde woanders sitzen. Aber gib mir bitte mei⬛ Lineal.

Jörg: Dei⬛ Lineal? Das ist doch nicht dei⬛ Lineal. Das ist mei⬛ Lineal. Dei⬛ Lineal ist auf Paulas Tisch.

Petra: Ach, richtig. Danke.

Jörg: Siehst du? Mädchen!! Außerdem, ist das dei⬛ Kuli?

Petra: Das ist doch kei⬛ Kuli, Idiot! Das is doch ei⬛ Bleistift.

Jörg: Na gut, ei⬛ Bleistift. Aber ist das dei⬛ Bleistift oder mei⬛ Bleistift?

Petra: Na, meiner, natürlich. Und jetzt Ruhe. Der Lehrer kommt.

Aufgabe Sechs

Can you have an argument with your partner about who owns what? How many things can you argue about? Stop arguing if your teacher says 'Ruhe bitte!'

Extension Three
Units 7–8

You already know something about the complications of German. You know that verbs change their endings, depending on who you are talking about. You know that nouns begin with a capital letter and that they have masculine, feminine, or neuter gender. You also know that the word in front of a noun may change its spelling, depending on the gender of the noun. You would have thought that would be enough, but unfortunately there are yet more complications to learn about. Remember, though, plenty of Germans get by without understanding anything about grammar, and even if you make mistakes, people will probably understand what you mean.

Accusative case

In German, the words for 'a', 'not a', 'my', and 'your' are not always **ein**, **kein**, **mein**, and **dein**. Look at this:

> **der Pullover**
> Das ist **mein** Pullover.
> Wo ist **mein** Pullover?
> **Mein** Pullover ist hier.
> Jan hat **meinen** Pullover an.

Which one is different?
Now look at this:

> **der Rock**
> Wo ist **dein** Rock?
> Anna hat **deinen** Rock an.
> Ist das **dein** Rock?
> Hier ist **dein** Rock.

Can you see the pattern?
If a masculine noun is at the beginning of a sentence, or near the end after **ist**, then you use **ein**, **kein**, **mein**, or **dein**. If it is near the end of a sentence after other verbs, use **einen**, **keinen**, **meinen** or **deinen**.

These forms are in the *accusative case*. Always use the accusative after **haben**, **habe**, **hast** and **hat** ('to have').

Aufgabe Eins

Complete the unfinished words. Some are accusative and others are not. All the nouns are masculine (**der**-words).

1. Dirk hat ei__ Pullover an.
2. Mei__ Pullover ist hier.
3. Maria hat dei__ Rock an.
4. Hat Michael dei__ Anorak an?
5. Wo ist mei__ Radiergummi?
6. Dei__ Bleistift ist auf dem Tisch.
7. Hier ist dei__ Anorak.
8. Heike hat kei__ Stuhl.
9. Jörg hat mei__ Bleistift.
10. Ich habe dei__ Kuli.

If the noun is not masculine, there is no problem with the accusative. Just use the normal word for 'a', 'not a', 'my' and 'your', in other words use **ein**, **kein**, **mein**, or **dein** with neuter nouns (**das**-words), and use **eine**, **keine**, **meine**, or **deine** with feminine nouns (**die**-words).

Aufgabe Zwei

Fill the gaps with a word for 'a', 'not a', 'my' or 'your'. You may choose any of these four, but make sure the ending is correct. You will have to check the gender of the noun in each sentence and then work out if it is in the accusative case or not. **Viel Spaß!** (Have fun!)

1. Ist das ____ Rock?
2. Wo ist ____ Kuli?
3. Karl hat ____ Buch.
4. Hier ist ____ Hose.
5. Martina hat ____ Heft.
6. ____ Jacke ist hier.
7. Das ist ____ Radiergummi.
8. Jochen, hast du ____ Hemd?

Aufgabe Drei

You've lent all your school things to your friends to get them out of trouble, and now you have nothing left for yourself. Tell your teacher why you haven't got these things:

Beispiel: Sabine — Sabine hat meinen Kuli.

1. Martina
2. Paul
3. Jochen
4. Anne
5. Rosemarie
6. Georg
7. Dieter
8. Silke
9. Claudia
10. Uwe

Aufgabe Vier

You have a German pen-friend who wants to know what a school uniform looks like. Write a short letter describing a photo of yourself in uniform. The German word is '**die Uniform**'.
You might write something like this:

> Lieber Joachim,
>   Das ist meine Uniform. Ich habe eine Hose an. Die Hose ist grau. Ich habe einen Pullover an. Der Pullover ist rot.

Remember to use the accusative after **habe**.

Extension Four
Units 9–10

If you did Exercise 4 in Extension Three, you probably found your letter very boring and repetitive because you did not know the word for 'it' in German. Now you can learn it.

There are several words for 'it'. Which one you use depends on whether the thing it refers to is a masculine, feminine, or neuter noun. Look at this:

> Where's John's bag?
> *It*'s here.
> 'It' refers to 'bag'.

Now look at some German examples.

Ist das Paulas Kuli?	Nein, **der** ist Peters.
Ist das deine Tasche?	Nein, **die** ist Wilhelms.
Ist das mein Buch?	Ja, **das** ist deins.

What is the word for 'it' that refers to masculine words?
How about feminine nouns? And neuter?

Aufgabe Eins

Put in the correct word for 'it' in each example.
1 Ist das dein Buch? Nein, ___ ist Peters.
2 Wo ist meine Tasche? ___ ist hier.
3 Wem gehört der Pullover? ___ ist Helgas.
4 Ist das mein Heft? Ja, ___ ist deins.
5 Wem gehört die Jacke? ___ ist Richards.
6 Wo ist dein Lineal? ___ ist in Hildas Tasche.

Aufgabe Zwei

Write six sentence pairs of your own on the same pattern as in the last exercise.

Aufgabe Drei

Do you remember how to say *where* things are? If not, look back to page 18. Then answer these questions, using the right word for 'it' each time.

1 Wo ist die Krawatte?
2 Wo ist der Pullover?
3 Wo ist das Lineal?
4 Wo ist der Kuli?
5 Wo ist die Tasche?

Now make up another five questions and answers and illustrate them.

Aufgabe Vier

Now you know how to say 'it' in German, you could improve the letter you wrote in Extension 3. Look at the letter on page 27. Write a similar letter to a pen-friend called Mark. You copy John's letter, but change the details. Say your name is Stefanie. You are sending a photo of yourself and your friend, Silke, which was taken in your classroom. In it, you are the one in blue trousers and a white jumper, while Silke is wearing a red dress. Ask Mark to send you a photo of himself in school uniform.

> **ACHTUNG!**
> *Boys* – sign yourselves **Dein** (+ *name*)
> *Girls* – sign yourselves **Deine** (+ *name*)

Aufgabe Fünf

Can you write a letter in German to a German pen-friend? Include a photo or drawing of yourself with a friend, and say what you are both wearing.

137

Extension Five
Unit 12

His and hers

| sein means 'his' | ihr means 'her' |

These words may change their spelling by adding the endings –e (for feminine nouns) and –en (for masculine nouns in the accusative case). They are just like **ein**, **kein**, **mein**, and **dein**.

Das ist Wolfgang.　Das ist **sein**　Vater.
　　　　　　　　　Das ist **seine**　Mutter.
　　　　　　　　　Das ist **sein**　Buch.
　　　　　　　　　Jan hat **seinen** Bleistift.

Das ist Sabine.　Das ist **ihr**　Bruder.
　　　　　　　　Das ist **ihre**　Schwester.
　　　　　　　　Das ist **ihr**　Lineal.
　　　　　　　　Jo　hat **ihren** Kuli.

Aufgabe Eins

Sort through Sabine and Wolfgang's possessions. Draw each pupil with his or her belongings, and write sentences using the above pattern to describe them. Choose the right word to mean 'his' or 'her' and check the ending carefully.

Der, die, das

How much do you remember about *gender* in German?

It means that nouns (naming words) are *masculine*, *feminine*, or *neuter*.
You cannot usually guess the gender of a noun.
When it is a person, you can generally guess the gender.

Masculine nouns are **der**-words.
Feminine nouns are **die**-words.
Neuter nouns are **das**-words.

These are some of the words we can put in front of a noun at the beginning of a sentence or after **ist**:

In front of masculine and neuter nouns:
ein, kein, mein, dein, sein, ihr

In front of feminine nouns:
eine, keine, meine, deine, seine, ihre

In front of masculine nouns in the accusative (e.g. after '**haben**') we can put these forms:

| einen | meinen | seinen |
| keinen | deinen | ihren |

Did you remember all that? Don't worry too much if you didn't – no one can remember everything!

Here is some more information about gender that you already know:

The word for 'it'
with masculine nouns is **der**.
with feminine nouns is **die**.
with neuter nouns is **das**.

The word for 'the' is the same.

der Vater	**die** Mutter	**das** Baby
der Bleistift	**die** Tasche	**das** Poster
der Rock	**die** Hose	**das** Hemd
der Tisch	**die** Mütze	**das** Buch

138

Aufgabe Zwei

Copy out the three lists above, putting the English meaning next to each noun. Add all the German nouns you know to the correct lists, with their meanings. Remember, if you can touch it, it's a noun! You should have at least 30 words altogether. Be sure to put the correct word for 'the' in front of each noun, and to begin each noun with a capital letter.

Aufgabe Drei

Look back to the letter on page 30. Write a similar letter in German describing a picture of your family. You can mention uncles, aunts, cousins and grandparents if you like, as well.

Extension Six
Unit 13

'To be' and 'to have'

Do you remember what a *verb* is? It's a *doing word*. Remember how the last few letters of a German verb have to be changed, depending on who you are talking about? Here's a reminder:

kommen	to come	
ich	komme	I come
du	kommst	you come
er		he
sie	kommt	she ⎱ comes
Name		name

As in English, some verbs do not follow the regular pattern. Look at these two:

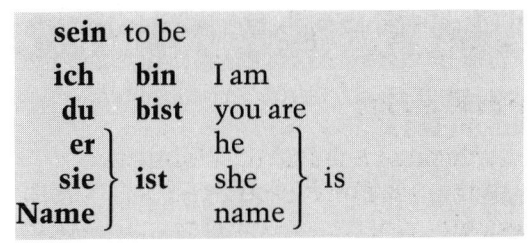

sein	to be	
ich	bin	I am
du	bist	you are
er		he
sie	ist	she ⎱ is
Name		name

haben	to have	
ich	habe	I have
du	hast	you have
er		he
sie	hat	she ⎱ has
Name		name

Aufgabe Eins

Complete the sentences below with the appropriate form of the verb **haben**.

1 Ich ___ mein Heft hier.
2 Du ___ aber eine schöne Tasche.
3 Er ___ kein Lineal.
4 Meine Tante ___ einen Bruder.
5 Das ist meine Schwester. Sie ___ einen neuen Freund.
6 Mein Vater ___ eine grüne Mütze.
7 ___ du Geschwister?
8 Ich ___ drei Schwestern aber keinen Bruder.

Aufgabe Zwei

Can you match the halves of the sentences below so that each sentence makes sense?

1 Wie alt bist   ist 14 Jahre alt.
2 Mein Bruder   ist deine Oma?
3 Ich   Manchester.
4 Frankfurt   du?
5 Wie alt   ist in Deutschland.
6 Sie ist   bin 19.
7 Wo ist   ist ein Kuli.
8 Er ist   bist in England.
9 Du   34.
10 Das   mein Vater.

Aufgabe Drei

Imagine your name is Regina. Write a letter in German to a pen-friend called Sandra. Describe how many brothers and sisters you have and say how old each one is. You have three brothers; Erik, Kai, and Sven, aged 16, 13, and 9. Your sister Gudrun is 15.

Aufgabe Vier

Write a letter to a German pen-friend describing your family and giving everyone's birthdays.

Extension Seven
Units 15–16

Plurals

Plural means more than one. In English it is very easy to form the plural of a noun. Most of the time, you just add –*s* to it.

   one boy → two boy*s*
   one cup → two cup*s*

In German it is a bit more complicated. Here are some rules to help you:

Most nouns ending in –**e** add the letter –**n** to form the plural.

Most nouns ending in –**t** add the letter –**e** to form the plural.

Singular	*Plural*
eine Flasche	zwei Flasche**n**
eine Tasse	zwei Tasse**n**
eine Torte	zwei Torte**n**
eine Tasche	zwei Tasche**n**

Singular	*Plural*
ein Wurstbrot	zwei Wurstbrot**e**
eine Bratwurst	zwei Bratwürst**e**
ein Brot	zwei Brot**e**
einen Wurst	zwei Würst**e**

Aufgabe Eins

Complete these sentences with the singular or the plural form of the unfinished word. Check that each sentence makes sense.

1 Was kostet eine Bratw__ bitte?
2 Zwei Ta__ Kaffee bitte.
3 Ich möchte bitte vier Käseb__.
4 Zwei Fl__ Limo bitte.
5 Was kostet ein Glas B__?
6 Meine Mutter und ich möchten zwei Curryw__.
7 Die Schinkenb__ sind hier teuer.
8 Eine T__ Tee bitte.

Aufgabe Zwei

What are they saying? Think up words to fill the speech bubbles in German.

'Is' and 'are'

If you use a noun in the plural, you may have to change the verb. We do this in English, too.

> My sister *is* a pest!
> My sisters *are* pests!
> That boy *dances* well.
> Those boys *dance* well.

Here are two German examples:

> *Singular:* Der Kaffee **ist** heiß.
> The coffee is hot.
> *Plural:* Die Kuchen **sind** gut.
> The cakes are good.

Aufgabe Drei

Make as many correct sentences as possible out of these sentence halves. You can use a phrase several times. Give yourself five minutes.

Die Flasche	ist nicht gut.
Die Brote	sind einfach Klasse!
Die Würste	ist kaputt.
Das Schinkenbrot	ist teuer.
Die Tassen	sind billig.
Die Currywurst	sind kalt.

Der, die, das, die

Have you noticed what the word for 'the' is with a plural noun? It is **die**, just as it is with the feminine singular. When a noun is plural, its gender does not make any difference. Look at this:

Singular	*Plural*
der Bleistift	**die** Bleistifte
die Wurst	**die** Würste
das Brot	**die** Brote
mein Bruder	**meine** Brüder
seine Schwester	**seine** Schwestern

141

Aufgabe Vier

Can you spot the plurals? Make a list. Look carefully at the last letters of each noun. You know what they should be, so if they have changed and have **die** in front, the noun must be in the plural form.

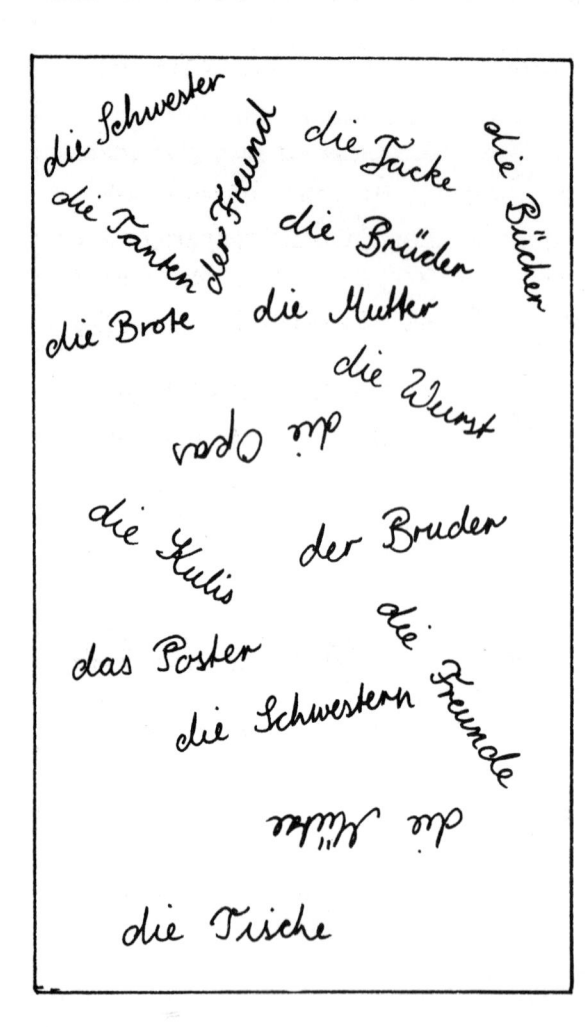

> die Schwester
> die Jacke
> die Tanten
> der Freund
> die Bücher
> die Brote
> die Brüder
> die Mutter
> die Wurst
> die Opas
> die Kulis
> der Bruder
> das Poster
> die Freunde
> die Schwestern
> die Mütter
> die Tische

Aufgabe Fünf

You're on a school trip to Germany, and the class has chosen you to give the order to the waiter. Choose from the menu on page 56.

> **ACHTUNG!**
> The plurals of **Kännchen**, **Glas** and **Stück** are the same as their singular forms.

Extension Eight
Units 17–19

More Verbs

trinken – *to drink*

This is a regular verb in the present tense. Work out the endings (look at page 123).

ich trink___
du trink___
er trink___
sie trink___
Anna trink___

essen – *to eat*

This is not so easy. There is a change of vowel in the verb after **du**, **er**, **sie**, or a name.

ich esse
du i**ß**t
er i**ß**t
sie i**ß**t
Jens i**ß**t

Aufgabe Eins

This grid shows you what different pupils like to eat and drink. The key is on the next page. Use the information to make 12 sentences saying what people like.

Beispiel: Jan trinkt sehr gern Kaffee.

	Kaffee	Tee	Apfelsaft	Currywurst	Trauben	Torte
Jan	✓✓	✗	✓	✓	✗✗	✗✗
Ulli	✗✗	✓✓	✓	✗	✓✓	✓
Fritz	✗	✓	✗✗	✓✓	✓✓	✓✓
Karin	✓✓	✓✓	✗	✓	✗	✓✓
Susanne	✓	✓✓	✓✓	✗✗	✗	✓✓
Thilo	✗✗	✗✗	✓	✓✓	✓	✗

√√√ = sehr gern . √√ = gern   √ = ganz gern
✗✗✗ = gar nicht gern   ✗✗ = nicht gern   ✗ = nicht sehr gern

Aufgabe Zwei

Read this letter, then match up the sentence halves below it.

> Lieber Jason,
> Du hast gefragt, was wir in Deutschland essen. Also bei meiner Familie ist das so:
> Um 7 Uhr gibt es Frühstück. Ich esse meistens ein Brötchen mit Wurst und trinke eine Tasse Kaffee. In der Schule ist um 10.30 Uhr Pause und da esse ich ein Käsebrot oder eine Banane oder einen Apfel. Mittagessen gibt es zu Hause um 1 Uhr. Wir essen warm; Gemüsesuppe, Fleisch, Kartoffeln und Salat.
> Kaffee und Kuchen gibt es um 4 Uhr. Aber ich esse Kuchen nicht gern. Um 7 Uhr gibt es Abendessen. Das ist immer kalt. Ich trinke gern Apfelsaft dazu und ich esse meistens Brot mit Schinken oder Käse. Im Winter trinke ich gern Tee.
> Was ißt Du in England? Gibt es bei Euch High Tea? Davon hat mir mein Englischlehrer erzählt.
> Schöne Grüße,
> Andreas

Match up:

1 Andreas ißt um   er eine Banane oder einen Apfel.
2 Er trinkt   gern Kuchen.
3 Um 10.30 Uhr ißt   sieben Uhr Frühstück.
4 Mittagessen gibt es   eine Tasse Kaffee.
5 Andreas ißt nicht   er Apfelsaft.
6 Zum Abendessen trinkt   um ein Uhr.

Aufgabe Drei

Try to write a letter to a German friend describing meals in your home. Follow the letter above very closely, just changing parts that do not apply to you.

Aufgabe Vier

Look at the menu on page 56. Make up a conversation in a café between two children asking each other what they like and deciding what to buy. Then make up a conversation between the two children and the waitress.

Extension Nine
Units 20–21

Dative case

Do you still remember what the accusative case is? It is when you have to make the following changes after **haben** (to have) and most other verbs apart from **sein** (to be).

ein	Kuli	Ich habe	**einen**	Kuli.
kein	Kuli	Petra hat	**keinen**	Kuli.
mein	Kuli	Jutta hat	**meinen**	Kuli.
der	Kuli	Hast du	**den**	Kuli?

There is another case in German, known as the *dative case*.
The accusative only affects masculine nouns, but the dative affects every gender. Look at these:

der Marktplatz
die Burg
das Rathaus

Die Post ist auf **dem** Marktplatz.
Das Museum ist in **der** Burg.
Das Hotel ist neben **dem** Rathaus.

You use the dative case after certain *prepositions*, that is to say, words that tell you the *position* of something.

Aufgabe Eins

Here is a list of prepositions you know. Copy them and fill in the meanings.

neben	hinter
in	vor
auf	zwischen
links von	zu
rechts von	gegenüber

Aufgabe Zwei

After **zu** (to) you need either **dem** (masculine and neuter) or **der** (feminine).
> **Zu dem** can be shortened to **zum**.
> **Zu der** can be shortened to **zur**.

Ask the way to the places listed.
– Wie komme ich am besten zum/zur ____?

1 das Rathaus
2 das Hotel Eden
3 der Bahnhof
4 die Burg
5 der Busbahnhof
6 das Museum
7 der Sportplatz
8 die Diskothek
9 der Marktplatz
10 die Pension Sonnenhof

Aufgabe Drei

Look at the map on page 60. Write at least ten sentences describing the position of buildings in the town. Check the gender of the nouns you use carefully, and be sure only to use the dative case after prepositions.

Beispiel:

Das Café   ist   **hinter der** Kirche.
(*not dative*)   (*dative*)

Aufgabe Vier

Write a letter to a German pen-friend describing where some of the important places in your home town are. You may include a map.

Extension Ten
Units 22–25

You, you, and you!

As you have already seen on page 64, there are three different words for 'you' in German. This actually makes things a lot easier, because people always know exactly who is being spoken to. However, as you might guess, there are also three different forms of the verb. You have seen two of them before:

du kommst	stem + st
ihr kommt	stem + t
Sie kommen	stem + en

kommen　**trinken**
du komm**st**　du trink**st**
ihr komm**t**　ihr trink**t**
Sie komm**en**　Sie trink**en**

heißen　**essen**
du heiß**t**　du iß**t**
ihr heiß**t**　ihr eß**t**
Sie heiß**en**　Sie ess**en**

Das ist anders:

haben　**sein**
du hast　du bist
ihr habt　ihr seid
Sie haben　Sie sind

Aufgabe Eins

Complete these sentences with the correct word for 'you'. Look carefully at the verb ending to decide what is correct.

1 Woher kommst ____?
2 Was trinkt ____ gern?
3 Was essen ____ gern?
4 Habt ____ meine Tasche?
5 Ißt ____ gern Fleisch?
6 Wie alt bist ____?
7 Hast ____ einen Kuli, bitte?
8 Wie heißt ____?
9 Haben ____ Käsebrot?
10 Sind ____ aus England?

Aufgabe Zwei

How would you address these people – **du**, **ihr**, or **Sie**?

Aufgabe Drei

Kim is not very good at getting her verb endings right, so she has deliberately smudged them so the teacher can't tell if they are right or wrong. Can you write out her work again, making all the endings clear? To help you, here's a chart:

ich –e		
du –st	ihr –t	
	Sie –en	
er –t		
sie –t		
Name –t		

Ich heiß● Kim Peddie. Ich bin vierzehn Jahre alt und ich wohn● in Rainham in Kent. Ich hab● zwei Brüder und eine Schwester. Meine Schwester heiß● Jean. Sie ist neunzehn. Sie wohn● auch in Rainham. Sie tanz● gern and geh● sehr gern schwimmen. Sie iß● gern Fisch mit Pommes Frites. Sie trink● gern Kaffee und Wein. Ich trink● auch gern Wein. Aber Bier trink● ich gar nicht gern. Mein Bruder Steve ist zweiundzwanzig Jahre alt. Er wohn● in London. Er ha● eine Freundin Paula. Steve geh● gern mit Paula ins Kino. Paula wohn● in Hemel Hempstead. Jeden Freitag fähr● Steve mit dem Zug nach Hemel. Er geht dann mit Paula in eine Diskothek. Geh● Sie auch gern tanzen?

Aufgabe Vier

Kim may not be very good at verb endings, but the rest of her work was very good. Can you write as much about your family and their likes and dislikes?

'Wollen' und 'möchten'

Here are two more verbs for you to learn. **Wollen** and **möchten** both mean 'want', but **möchten** is more polite and can be translated as 'would like'. These two verbs are called *modal verbs*. Modal verbs are irregular. Firstly, there is often a different vowel in the stem of the verb in the singular:

Singular	*Plural*
ich will	
du willst	ihr wollt
er will	Sie wollen
sie will	
Vowel **i**	*Vowel* **o**

Secondly, the ending after **er** and **sie** does not follow the usual pattern. Normally, you expect the ending **–t** after **er** and **sie**:

Regular verbs	*Modal verbs*
er kommt	er **will**
sie heißt	sie **möchte**
Petra trinkt	Gabi **kann**

	Plural	
First person	**wir kaufen**	we buy
Second person	**ihr kauft** **Sie kaufen**	you buy you buy
Third person	**sie kaufen**	they buy

Man ist neu. **Man** heißt 'one' auf englisch.

Aufgabe Zwei

Write out the following verbs in all their forms with the meaning of each form in English.

1 kommen
2 trinken
3 gehen
4 heißen (⚡ watch out with **du**)
5 essen   (⚡ watch out with **du**, **er** and **sie** singular)

Extension Thirteen
Unit 34

> Lieber Jason,
> Wie schön, daß Du uns besuchen kommst! Wie Du weißt, wohne ich in der Bäckerei mit meiner Familie. Das sind noch einmal meine Mutter, mein Vater und meine Schwester. Meine Schwester heißt Sonia und sie ist 7 Jahre alt.
> Unsere Bäckerei ist auf dem Marktplatz gleich hinter dem Kino, gegenüber dem Hotel Krone. Das ist ganz einfach zu finden. Vom Bahnhof fährst Du mit dem Bus Linie 13 bis zum Marktplatz, und von der Haltestelle sind es noch etwa zwanzig Meter.
> Ich warte an der Haltestelle auf Dich. Oder, wenn Du vom Bahnhof aus telefonierst, kann Mutti Dich mit dem Auto abholen. Ich bin leider noch in der Schule, wenn Dein Zug ankommt. Unsere Telefonnummer ist (06133 - Vorwahl) 2651.
> Bis bald.
> Schöne Grüße,
> Andreas

Aufgabe Eins

Read Andreas' letter and answer these questions:

1 What is Jason planning to do?
2 How many people are in Andreas' family?

3 What is the family business?
4 Where exactly do they live?
5 How would you get there from the station?
6 Is Andreas' house far from the bus stop?
7 Where will Andreas wait?
8 Why could Jason phone?

Aufgabe Zwei

Think up words to fill the speech bubbles in German.

Extension Fourteen
Units 35–36

Ulm, den 23. August

Liebe Uschi,

Hier ist eine Liste von Andenken, die Du aus England mitbringen sollst. Also, zuerstmal für Tanja kaufe bitte eine Schallplatte oder noch besser eine Kassette, die kannst Du besser transportieren. Für Dieter vielleicht etwas mit Fußball, ein Hemd oder einen Schal. Du weißt ja, er mag Doncaster Rovers am liebsten. Oma möchte gerne echt englischen Tee. Ich glaube, ein Pfund ist genug. Für Deinen Vater etwas Süßes, Bonbons oder Schokolade, eine große Dose bitte. Und ich möchte gern ein schönes T-Shirt mit der englischen Flagge.

Hier sind noch hundert Mark extra für die Geschenke. Ich hoffe, das ist genug.

Viel Spaß meine Kleine.
Komm gesund wieder.
Alles Liebe
Deine Mutti

P.S. Vergiß nicht Deinen Tanten eine Postkarte zu schicken.

Aufgabe Eins

Wer bekommt was?
Antworte auf deutsch

Tanja?   Vati?
Dieter?   Mutti?
Oma?   Tanten?

Hat Uschi genug Geld?

Aufgabe Zwei

Imagine you are Uschi. Reply to your mother's letter (above), saying what you are buying for whom.

> ⚡ If you say you are buying something which is masculine in gender, you have to use the accusative. Remember?
> Look:
>   Ich kaufe ein T-shirt für dich (= *for you*)
>   Ich kaufe eine Kassette für Tanja.
>   Ich kaufe **einen** Schal für Dieter.

> ⚡ If you would not say 'a' or 'an' in English, you don't need to worry about this:
>   Ich kaufe Rasierwasser für Onkel Fritz.
>   Ich kaufe Postkarten für Tante Gisela.

Extension Fifteen
Unit 41

'Mögen' und 'können'

Here are two more *modal verbs*, similar to **wollen**. Remember that in modal verbs there is often a different vowel in the singular from the one in the infinitive. Also, the **er** and **sie** forms are the same as the **ich** form.

mögen – to like

ich	mag	wir	mögen
du	magst	ihr	mögt
		Sie	mögen
er	mag	sie	mögen
sie	mag		
es	mag		
man	mag		

Vowel **a**   Vowel **ö**

können – to be able

ich	kann	wir	können
du	kannst	ihr	könnt
		Sie	können
er	kann	sie	können
sie	kann		
es	kann		
man	kann		

Vowel **a**   Vowel **ö**

Did you notice an extra verb form?

Es usually means 'it', but only when you are referring to a neuter noun. You will find out more about this in Unit 45. The verb form for **es** is always exactly the same as the form for **er**. As you know, you can also use **der**, **die** and **das** to mean 'it'. The verb form is the same as with **es**.

Have you noticed anything about the word **sie**?
It can mean three things – 'she', 'you' (polite form) or 'they'. How confusing! How can you tell which is intended?

If **sie** means 'she', the verb form will be the same as with **er**.
If **sie** means 'they', the verb form will be the infinitive.
If **Sie** means 'you', there will be a capital letter.

Aufgabe Eins

Write the meaning of **sie/Sie** in each sentence.

1. Haben Sie Käsebrot?
2. Kann sie schwimmen?
3. Ich habe zwei Brüder, sie heißen Jens und Lutz.
4. Das ist meine Schwester. Sie ist 8 Jahre alt.
5. Wie komme ich zum Rathaus?
   Sie fahren mit dem Bus.
6. Ist Sabine hier?
   Nein, sie ist heute nicht in der Schule.
7. Sagen Sie bitte, ist hier eine Toilette?

Aufgabe Zwei

Write out the modal verbs **wollen** and **möchten** in all the present tense forms, following the models given above.

Aufgabe Drei

Complete the following sentences with appropriate verbs in the correct form. They are all in the plural.

1. Meine Schwestern ____ Klara und Elisabeth.
2. Wir ____ immer mit dem Bus zur Schule.
3. Meine Schwester und ich ____ Englisch sehr gern.
4. Ihr ____ schon wieder die Deutschhefte vergessen?
5. Wann ____ ihr in Frankfurt an?
6. Wir ____ morgen vielleicht Badminton spielen.
7. Was ____ ihr für eure Mutter?
8. Was ____ ihr trinken?
9. Mein Freund und ich ____ sehr gern Pommes frites.
10. Wohin ____ wir fahren?

Extension Sixteen
Units 42–45

Aufgabe Eins

Here are a number of sentences. Some describe Sebastian, a boy, while others describe Sabrina, a girl. Sort them into two groups and copy them out. Then try to draw them both.

Ihr Haar ist halblang.
Er heißt Sebastian.
Sie heißt Sabrina.
Er ist 1,92 m groß.
Sein Haar ist braun.
Er ist ziemlich schlank.
Sein Haar ist lockig.
Sie ist schlank.
Sie ist 1,70 m groß.
Ihre Augen sind grün.
Ihr Haar ist mittelblond.
Er hat blaugraue Augen.
Sie hat einen Pullover und Jeans an.
Er hat einen Pullover und Jeans an.

Aufgabe Zwei

Imagine you are meeting your pen-friend for the first time. He or she has sent you the following description:

> Ich bin 14 Jahre alt, ungefähr 1,65 m groß und sehr schlank. Mein Haar ist hellbraun, ziemlich kurz und lockig. Meine Augen sind grünbraun. Ich habe einen Anorak, Jeans und blauweiße Sportschuhe an. Ich habe eine Brille auf.

Would you recognize him or her? If not, what other information would you want? Write a description of yourself in German as you are now, giving as many details as possible.

German-English Vocabulary

Here is an alphabetical list of all the German words you will find in this book with their English translation. The gender is given for nouns and the plural form if you are likely to want to use it. The plural form is in brackets after the noun. Here are some examples of how to use the information:

Singular	Plural
das **Kino** (–s)	die **Kinos**
der **Film** (–e)	die **Filme**
das **Kind** (–er)	die **Kinder**
der **Hamster** (–)	die **Hamster**
das **Buch** (¨-er)	die **Bücher**

der **Abend** evening.
abends in the evening
aber but
die **Abfahrt** departure
das **Abzeichen** (–) transfer, badge
acht eight
Achtung! caution!
achtzehn eighteen
achtzig eighty
die **Adresse** address
alt old
die **Ampel** traffic lights
an on
anders different
angeln to fish
die **Ankunft** arrival
der **Anorak** (–s) anorak
die **Antwort** (–en) answer
antworten to answer
der **Apfelsaft** apple juice
die **Apotheke** chemist's
die **Apothekerin** chemist (woman)
April April
auch too
auf on, in, open
auf Wiedersehen goodbye
das **Auge** eye
August August
aus from
das **Auto** (–s) car

der **Automechaniker** car mechanic (man)
die **Bäckerei** baker's
die **Bäckerin** baker (woman)
das **Bad** bathroom
der **Bahnhof** station
der **Balkon** balcony
die **Banane** (–n) banana
der **Bankbeamte** bank clerk (man)
die **Banknote** (–n) banknote
basteln to make models
die **Bedienung** service
beginnen to begin
der **Behälter** (–) container
bei with, at
das **Bein** (–e) leg
das **Beispiel** (–e) example
bekommen to get
belegtes Brot sandwich
besonders especially
am **besten** best
das **Bett** (–en) bed
das **Bier** beer
das **Bild** (–er) picture
billig cheap
ich **bin** am
Biologie biology
bis zu up to
du **bist** you are
bitte please; here you are; can you repeat that?

blau blue
der **Bleistift** (–e) pencil
die **Bluse** (–n) blouse
der **Boden** floor
der **Bonbon** (–s) sweet
braun brown
der **Briefkasten** postbox
die **Briefmarke** (–n) stamp
die **Brille** glasses
das **Brot** bread
das **Brötchen** (–) bread roll
der **Bruder** (¨) brother
das **Buch** (¨-er) book
buchstabieren to spell
bunt coloured
das **Büro** office
der **Bus** bus
die **Bushaltestelle** bus stop
die **Butter** butter
das **Café** café
Chemie chemistry
die **Cola** (–s) coca cola
der **Cousin** (–s) cousin (boy)
die **Cousine** (–n) cousin (girl)

da there
danke thank you
danke schön many thanks
dann then
das that/the
das **Datum** date
dein your

153

denn then
deutsch German
Deutschland Germany
Dezember December
der **Dialog** (–e) dialogue
dich you
dick fat
Dienstag Tuesday
dir (to) you
die **Direktorin** headmistress
die **Disco** (–s) disco
die **Diskothek** (–en) discotheque
doch! oh yes (it is)!
Donnerstag Thursday
doof stupid
das **Doppelhaus** semi-detached house
dort there
die **Dose** (–n) tin
dreh dich um turn round
drei three
dreißig thirty
dreizehn thirteen
der **dritte** the third
die **Drogerie** chemist's
der **Drogist** chemist (man)
drüben over there
du you
dunkel dark

die **Ecke** corner
das **Ei** (–er) egg
ein a, an, one
einfach one way
einfach Klasse! simply great!
das **Einfamilienhaus** detached house
einige some

einmal once
eins one
das **Einzelkind** only child

das **Eis** ice cream
elf eleven
englisch English
entlang along
Entschuldigung excuse me
er he
das **Erdgeschoß** ground floor
Erdkunde geography
erfinden to invent
erst first
es gibt there is
essen to eat
etwas something
das **Eßzimmer** dining-room

die **Fabrik** factory
das **Fach** (¨–er) subject
fahren to travel
falsch false
die **Familie** family
fang an! start!
die **Farbe** (–n) colour
Februar February
feiern to celebrate
das **Fell** hair/coat
das **Fenster** (–) window
der **Fernseher** TV set
fernsehen to watch television
das **Fest** celebration
der **Film** (–e) film
finden to find
die **Flasche** (–n) bottle
das **Fleisch** meat
die **Fleischerei** butcher's
der **Flur** hall
das **Foto** (–s) photo
fotografieren to take photos
fragen to ask
französisch French
die **Frau** (–en) Mrs, Ms, woman
das **Fräulein** Miss, Ms, young woman
Freitag Friday

der **Freund** (e–) friend (boy)
die **Freundin** (–nen) friend (girl)
freundlich friendly
das **Frühstück** breakfast
fünf five
fünfzehn fifteen
fünfzig fifty
zu **Fuß** on foot
der **Fußball** football
die **Fußgängerzone** pedestrian precinct

ganz quite
gar nicht not at all
gebrochen broken
der **Geburtstag** birthday
gegenüber opposite
gehen to go
gehört belongs to
gelb yellow
das **Geld** money
das **Gemüse** vegetables
der **Gemüsehändler** greengrocer (man)
der **Gemüseladen** greengrocer's
genau exactly
gern like
die **Gesamtschule** comprehensive school
das **Geschenk** (–e) present
Geschichte history
es **gibt** there is
das **Glas** (–) glass
der **Goldfisch** (–e) goldfish
grau grey
groß big
grün green
die **Grundschule** primary school
der **Gruß** (¨–e) greeting
die **Größe** size
gut good, well
das **Gymnasium** grammar school

ich **habe** I have
haben to have
das **Hähnchen** chicken
hallo hello
die **Haltestelle** stop
der **Hamster** (–) hamster
der **Handschuh** (–e) glove
du **hast** you have
er **hat** he has
der **Hauptbahnhof** main station
das **Haus** (¨-er) house
Hauswirtschaft home economics
das **Heft** (–e) exercise book
heißen to be called
helfen to help
hell light
das **Hemd** (–en) shirt
der **Herr** (–en) Mr, man
heute today
hier here
hin there
hin und zurück return (ticket)
hinter behind
das **Hobby** (–s) hobby
hör auf! stop!
hör zu! listen!
die **Hose** trousers
das **Hotel** (–s) hotel
der **Hund** (–e) dog
hundert hundred

ich I
Ihnen you
ihr you, her
die **Imbißstube** snack bar
in in
inbegriffen included
interessant interesting
das **Interview** interview
Irland Ireland
ist is
ißt eat, eats

ja yes
die **Jacke** jacket
das **Jahr** (–e) year
... Jahre alt ... years old
Januar January
die **Jeans** jeans
jeder every
jetzt now
der **Joghurt** yogurt
die **Jugendherberge** youth hostel
Juli July
Juni June

der **Kaffee** coffee
der **Kakao** cacoa
das **Kaninchen** (–) rabbit
kann can
das **Kännchen** pot
die **Kantine** canteen
das **Kanu** canoe
kaputt broken
die **Kartoffel** (–n) potato
der **Käse** cheese
das **Käsebrot** (–e) cheese sandwich
die **Kassette** (–n) cassette
die **Katze** (–n) cat
kaufen to buy
das **Kaufhaus** (¨-er) store
kein no, none
der **Kellner** waiter
die **Kellnerin** waitress
die **Kette** (–n) necklace
das **Kilo** kilogram
das **Kilometer** (–) kilometre
das **Kind** (–er) child
der **Kindergarten** nursery
das **Kino** (–s) cinema
die **Kirche** church
die **Klasse** (–n) class
Klasse! first class, great!
das **Klassenzimmer** classroom

das **Kleid** (–er) dress
Kleider clothes
der **Kleiderschrank** wardrobe
klein small
kochen to cook
kommen to come
kommt an arrives
die **Konditorei** cake shop
können can
die **Kosmetik** cosmetics
kosten to cost
die **Krawatte** (–n) tie
die **Kreuzung** crossroads
die **Küche** kitchen
der **Kuchen** (–) cake
der **Kuli** (–s) ballpoint
der **Kunde** (–n) customer (*man*)
die **Kundin** (–nen) customer (*woman*)
Kunst art
kurz short

die **Lampe** (–n) light
lang long
langsam slow
langweilig boring
Latein Latin
laufen to walk
laut loud
lauter louder
das **Lebensmittelgeschäft** grocery store
die **Lebensmittel** groceries
die **Lederjacke** (–n) leather jacket
die **Lehrer** (–) teacher (*man*)
die **Lehrerin** (–nen) teacher (*woman*)
leicht easy
leise quiet
lesen to read
lieb dear
das **Lieblingsfach** (¨-er) favourite subject

die **Limonade** lemonade
das **Lineal** (–e) ruler
die **Linie** (–n) number (*of bus*)
links left
das **Liter** (–) litre
lockig curly

mach auf/zu! open/close!
machen to do
mag like
Mai May
der **Main** River Main
malen to paint
man one, you, they
die **Mark** (–) mark
der **Marktplatz** market place
die **Marmelade** jam
März March
Mathe maths
die **Maus** (¨-e) mouse
die **Medizin** medicine
das **Meerschweinchen** (–) guinea pig
mehr more
die **Mehrwertsteuer** VAT
die **Meile** (–n) mile
mein my
das **Meter** (–) metre
die **Metzgerei** butcher's
die **Metzgerin** butcher (*woman*)
die **Milch** milk
mit with, by
mittags at lunchtime
mittel medium
Mittwoch Wednesday
möchten would like
mögen to like
der **Monat** month
Montag Monday
der **Morgen** morning
morgens in the morning

die **Mosel** River Moselle
das **Motorrad** motorbike
die **Münze** (–n) coin
das **Museum** museum
die **Mutter** mother
Mutti Mum
die **Mütze** (–n) hat

na well
nach to
nachmittags in the afternoon
der **nächste** the nearest
die **Nacht** night
nachts at night
der **Nachttisch** (–e) bedside table
der **Name** (–n) name
Naturwissenschaft science
natürlich of course
neben next to
nein no
neu new
neun nine
neunzehn nineteen
neunzig ninety
nicht not
nichts nothing
noch even
Nord North
November November
null nought
die **Nummer** (–n) number
nur only

Herr **Ober!** waiter!
das **Obst** fruit
oder or
Oktober October
die **Oma** (–s) granny
der **Onkel** (–) uncle
der **Opa** (–s) grandad
orange orange
der **Orangensaft** orange juice
Ost East

Österreich Austria

das **Paar** pair
das **Paket** (–e) parcel
das **Parfum** perfume
der **Park** park
der **Partner** (–) partner (*boy*)
die **Partnerin** (–nen) partner (*girl*)
die **Party** party
passen to fit
die **Pension** bed & breakfast
der **Pfennig** (–) pfennig
das **Pferd** (–e) horse
der **Pfirsich** (–e) peach
das **Pflaster** plaster
das **Pfund** (–) pound
Physik physics
die **Platte** (–n) record
der **Plattenspieler** record player
der **Platz** square
Politik politics
Pommes frites chips
die **Portion** (–en) portion
die **Post** post office
das **Poster** (–) poster
die **Postkarte** (–n) postcard
Pralinen chocolates
der **Pullover** (–) pullover

radfahren to cycle
der **Radiergummi** (–s) rubber
das **Radio** (–s) radio
das **Rasierwasser** aftershave
das **Rathaus** town hall
die **Realschule** secondary school
Rechnen arithmetic
rechts right
das **Regal** shelves
das **Reihenhaus** terraced house
reiten to ride

156

der **Rhein** River Rhine
richtig true
der **Rock** (¨-e) skirt, kilt
der **Rollstuhl** wheelchair
rot red
Ruhe! silence!

die **S-Bahn** suburban railway
Sachkunde humanities
der **Saft** juice
sag mal tell me
der **Salat** salad
das **Salz** salt
Samstag Saturday
die **Sandale** (–n) sandal
die **Schachtel** (–n) box
die **Schallplatte** (–n) record
das **Schiff** ship
der **Schinken** ham
schlafen to sleep
das **Schlafzimmer** bedroom
schlank slim
das **Schloß** castle
schnell quick
die **Schokolade** chocolate
Schottland Scotland
der **Schrank** (¨-e) cupboard
schreiben to write
der **Schuh** (–e) shoe
die **Schule** (–n) school
schwarz black
die **Schweiz** Switzerland
schwer hard
die **Schwester** (–n) sister
das **Schwimmbad** swimming pool
schwimmen to swim
der **Schüler** (–) pupil
sechs six
sechzehn sixteen

sechzig sixty
sehen to see
sehr very
sein his
senden to send
September September
der **Sessel** (–) armchair
setz dich! sit down!
das **Shampoo** shampoo
sicher sure
Sie you
sie she, they
sieben seven
siebzehn seventeen
siebzig seventy
sind are
singen to sing
so so
die **Socke** (–n) ankle sock
das **Sofa** sofa
sogar even
Sonntag Sunday
die **Sozialkunde** social studies
die **Soße** gravy, sauce
der **Spaß** fun
spät late
wie **spät ist es?** what's the time?
die **Speisekarte** menu
spielen to play
der **Spitzer** (–) pencil sharpener
das **Sportzentrum** sports centre
sprechen to speak
der **Sprudel** mineral water
die **Stadt** town
steh auf! stand up!
Stelzen stilts
die **Stereoanlage** stereo
der **Sticker** (–) badge
der **Stiefel** (–) boot
der **Stock** floor
die **Straße** (–n) road
die **Straßenbahn** tram

das **Streichholz** (¨-er) match
stricken to knit
der **Strumpf** (¨-e) long sock, stocking
die **Strumpfhose** tights
der **Stuhl** (¨-e) chair
der **Stundenplan** timetable
Stunk trouble
das **Stück** (–) piece
Süd South
der **Supermarkt** supermarket
die **Suppe** soup
die **Tablette** (-n) tablet
die **Tafel** board
der **Tag** (–e) day
die **Tante** (–n) aunt
tanzen to dance
die **Tasche** (–n) bag
die **Tasse** (–n) cup
tausend thousand
der **Tee** tea
das **Telefon** telephone
telefonieren to phone
der **Teller** (–) plate
der **Teppich** (–e) carpet
teuer expensive
das **Tier** (–e) pet, animal
der **Tisch** (–e) table
der **Titel** title
die **Toilette** (–n) toilet
die **Tomate** (–n) tomato
die **Torte** (–n) fruit flan
die **Traube** (–n) grape
trinken to drink
Tschüs goodbye
es **tut mir leid** sorry
die **Tür** door
die **Tüte** (–n) bag
typisch typical

die **U-Bahn** underground
übernachten to spend the night

157

    ...Uhr ...o'clock
    um at
    und and
    ungefähr about
die **Uniform** uniform

der **Vater** father
    vergessen to forget
das **Verkehrsamt** tourist office
der **Verkäufer** (–) salesman
    verschieden various
    verstehen to understand
das **Videogerät** video recorder
    viel lots of
    vier four
    vierzehn fourteen
    vierzig forty
    violett purple
    vollschlank plump
    von of
    vor in front of
der **Vorhang** (¨-e) curtain
    vormittags in the morning

    wann when
    war was
    Waren stock
    warst were
    was? what?
der **Wein** wine
    weit far
    weiß white
ich **weiß nicht** I don't know
    welch which
der **Wellensittich** (–e) budgerigar
    wem? to whom?
    wen? whom?
    wer? who?
    werden to become
    Werken craft
    West West
    wie? how? what?
    wie geht's? how are you?
    wieder again
auf **Wiedersehen** goodbye
    wiederholen to repeat
    wieviel? how much?
    wieviele? how many?
den **wievielten?** what date?
    will want, wants

    wir we
    wo? where?
    woher? from where?
    wohin? where to?
der **Wohnblock** block of flats
    wohnen to live
der **Wohnort** residence
die **Wohnung** flat
das **Wohnzimmer** lounge
    wollen to want
die **Wurst** sausage
die **Wüstenratte** (–n) gerbil

    zahlen to pay
    zehn ten
    zeichnen to draw
    ziemlich quite
    zu to; too; shut
    zu Hause at home
der **Zucker** sugar
der **Zug** train
    zurück back
    zwanzig twenty
    zwei two
    zweimal twice, two
der **zweite** second
    zwischen between
    zwölf twelve